Hc

Aarti Kelshikar is an intercultural consultant and coach with over fifteen years of work experience in India, Singapore and the Philippines.

She is a certified facilitator of Cultural Intelligence from the Cultural Intelligence Center in the US. She is also a certified executive coach from the international Neuro Leadership group. Since 2008, she has been associated with two US-based global mobility companies, for which she has delivered customized intercultural training programmes for professionals relocating worldwide. She has trained senior executives from multinational corporations like Nestlé, Unilever, Proctor and Gamble, Colgate Palmolive, and Texas Instruments. She is also a consultant with a leadership development company in India, for which she has conducted workshops on building a global mindset and enhancing executive presence.

Before discovering the fascinating world of intercultural coaching, she worked for seven years in the area of securities market compliance with the Securities and Exchange Board of India in Mumbai and with a consulting firm in Singapore.

Aarti has a master's in business administration from the Narsee Monjee Institute of Management Studies and a bachelor's in commerce from Sydenham College in Mumbai. She enjoys travelling and reading. She lives in Mumbai with her husband and daughter.

HOW INDIA WORKS

MAKING SENSE OF A COMPLEX
CORPORATE CULTURE

Aarti Kelshikar

HARPER
BUSINESS

An Imprint of HarperCollins Publishers

First published in India in 2018 by Harper Business
An imprint of HarperCollins *Publishers*
A-75, Sector 57, Noida, Uttar Pradesh 201301, India
www.harpercollins.co.in

2 4 6 8 10 9 7 5 3 1

P-ISBN: 978-93-5277-771-6
E-ISBN: 978-93-5277-772-3

Typeset in 11/15 Sabon LT Std at
Manipal Digital Systems, Manipal

Printed and bound at
Thomson Press (India) Ltd

For Anushka,
as she embarks on a whole new journey across cultures

Contents

Foreword

From the sights and sounds to the tastes and textures, the experience of working and living in 'Incredible India' can be both enthralling and mystifying.

But this can be the case, in varying degrees, in any unfamiliar or different place or culture. Let me share a personal anecdote. As a young couple, my wife and I were transported from Mumbai to the cold climes of North Yorkshire in the UK way back in the mid-1980s. You can imagine the culture shock; even the language – supposedly English – was spoken in a very strong Geordie accent, which we could barely decipher. I told my boss at ICI (Imperial Chemical Industries) that this was a 'hardship posting' for me – as I have to wash my own dishes, do the laundry and ironing, mow the lawns and hoover the house weekly. Talk of challenges of living in a developed country! We had to grow out of the habit of always having house help, whom we were so used to back home, and decided to do in Rome as the Romans do. Then onwards, we moved from surviving to thriving.

The experience above relates to the personal aspect of life in a different land. One of the biggest challenges when working with a set of different people or in a different country is the cultural variation. All cultures have their own norms, values, beliefs and practices, which are similar to none.

In my professional experience of working with a Swiss company for more than twenty years, I have seen first-hand the importance of having a strong cultural quotient. One of the earliest things I learnt was that while openness towards technology and innovation gave the Swiss an air of daring-do, one should not be misled. The Swiss by nature are conservative, empirical-minded and prefer to stick to rules. Fuzzy logic has no place in their thinking. Meetings cannot be held spontaneously. If you come to the meeting on time, you are late because you should have arrived a few minutes earlier so that the meeting could 'start on time'. Well, this holds true for social occasions too. You can imagine the consternation of a colleague of mine when he arrived half an hour late for a dinner at a Swiss colleague's home and was told he would have to skip the drinks as the roast was ready in the microwave for serving! I am sure a large number of harried housewives in India would love to do the same but the spiritual quotient in them militates against this Swiss norm. Of course, one must not forget that the Swiss are very private people and it is taboo to ask any personal questions – which we tend to do in India at the drop of a hat!

As the world gets better connected and as intercultural interactions increase, one finds that the challenges and complexities also increase. And when one is talking about a country like India, the complexities are manifold. India is not one country but many countries rolled into one. Whichever way you look at it, the prospect of living and working here and dealing with its unmatched diversity and contrasting character is complex at many levels. Like ebony and ivory on a piano, Indians (mostly) live together in harmony and even play a common melody together.

Given the vast numbers of Indians both in India and abroad and the attractiveness of the growing Indian economy, working with Indians is inevitable for many in business the world over. People have questions – asked aloud and wondered privately – about the what, how and why of Indian behaviours and mindsets. Here, 'yes' may mean 'no' and 'no' may mean 'yes' depending on the way one interprets the nod or shake of the head in response to one's questions! This is one of the many nuances that Aarti Kelshikar explores in *How India Works: Making Sense of a Complex Corporate Culture.*

Drawing on her experience of and exposure to intercultural understanding, she takes us on a journey that navigates the landscape of cultural complexities in India. Aarti has lucidly woven her views and experiences along with those of sixty professionals – both Indians and expats who have lived and worked in India. It is a treat to read all their stories, unique in their own way, and to see their journeys through their eyes.

While expats stand to benefit from reading this book, it is particularly relevant for Indian readers. In his book *Cultural DNA: The Psychology of Globalization*, Gurnek Bains highlights how, as per research conducted, 34 per cent of Indians had a development need around self-awareness, the highest percentage of all global regions. An area that this is often manifested in is the manner in which Indians accept feedback (which is also discussed later in the book). *How India Works* provides an opportunity for Indians to be more cognizant of their behaviours, their strengths and their idiosyncrasies.

Everything in India happens in the richness and fullness of time, and as Sonny in the movie *The Best Exotic Marigold Hotel* tells a disappointed tourist, 'In India we have a saying: "Everything will be all right in the end." So if it's not all right, it is not yet the end.' For those willing to immerse themselves in the paradox that is India and be patient to explore the layers of cultural complexity, the 'end' will be a rich and rewarding journey – both on the professional and personal fronts. *How India Works* can be a good guide on this journey; do savour and enjoy it!

Ranjit Shahani
Vice-Chairman and Managing Director,
Novartis India Ltd, 2002–18
June 2018

A List of People Quoted in the Book

This is a list of the people quoted in this book. The complete list of people interviewed is given under Acknowledgements. All of the following are/were based in India and their designations are as at the time of interviewing them.

- Amit Agarwal, Vice-President and Country Leader, Thermo Fisher Scientific
- Sateen Bailur, Senior Manager at a large foreign bank
- Gaurav Bhatiani, senior infrastructure professional with experience in policy, financing and strategy
- Martin Bienz, Consul General of Switzerland
- Josh Bishop, High School Principal, American School of Bombay
- Brendon Breen, Health Teacher and Technology Coach at an international school
- Peter Clark, Chief Operating Officer for a large foreign company

- Susanne Cox, Senior HR Manager at an Indian petrochemicals organization
- Sven De Wachter, Director of Wachter Oriental
- Nishith Desai, international lawyer and globalization expert
- Mary Kay Hoffman, international school educator
- Virginia Holmes, Director, Fat Mu
- Jos Hulsbosch, Chief Operations Officer, Union Kbc Asset Management
- Bernard Imhasly, former Swiss diplomat and foreign correspondent
- Craig Johnson, Head of School, American School of Bombay
- Justin, Manager from New Zealand
- Jaideep Kalgutkar, General Manager at a large IT company
- Madhav Kalyan, MD & CEO, JPMorgan Chase Bank N.A., India
- Chloe Kannan, international school teacher
- Rajan Khorana, former director at a large US-based financial institution
- Nick Kilstein, international school teacher
- Yuk Dong Kim, CEO, Shinhan Bank, India
- Joe King, Head, Audi, India
- Stans Kleijnen, Executive Director, Netherlands Foreign Investment Agency, India
- Eric Labartette, Managing Director, Metro One Operation
- Lorna, South African expat
- Shanti Mohan, Co-founder and CEO, LetsVenture
- Rory Newcomb, international school teacher
- Jeetu Panjabi, part of senior management at a large global financial company

- Nimesh Rathod, Business Acumen specialist
- Chris Rogers, Senior Executive of a large multinational financial services company
- Anand Sanghi, President, Asia Market at Vertiv
- Hari Sankaran, Vice Chairman, IL&FS Group
- Amy Sebes, teacher at an international school and spouse of a former US Consul General
- Ali Sleiman, General Manager of a multinational pharmaceutical organization
- Kanchana TK, Director General, Organization of Pharmaceutical Producers of India (OPPI)
- Carrie Udeshi, Intercultural Consultant
- Richard van der Merwe, Senior Director at a large life sciences company in India
- Aditi Vijayakar, repatriate
- Ashish Vijayakar, Senior Officer at a foreign bank

Where names have been changed:

- David, Swiss expat who has worked in different roles and assignments in India
- James, Executive with a multinational healthcare company
- Kevin, Asian expat
- Meera, corporate lawyer
- Mukesh, Senior Executive at a large American organization
- Pranav, part of the senior management at a multinational bank
- Rajesh, Managing Director of a large multinational organization

- Ryan, Senior Executive of an Indo-German insurance start-up
- Sangeeta, HR director at a multinational organization
- Scott, Senior Executive at a multinational organization
- Shashi, Executive at a financial institution
- Simon, British expat

The following shared a few quotes and anecdotes:

- Parag Jain, Compliance Consultant
- Fiona Reynolds, experienced international educator

Introduction

'Have you lost your mind?!'

Andy was amazed that his wife Sarah would even consider leaving their comfortable (for the most part) suburban life in Boston for an overseas assignment.

And to India, of all places!

For many companies, a posting to India is now fairly de rigueur in order to give their executives exposure and experience of working in an emerging market that has the numbers in terms of size of population, steady economic growth, a burgeoning middle class and one of the largest under-the-age-of-35 populace. (To digress slightly, as per the HSBC Expat Explorer 2016 report,* 'Three in five or 60 per cent of expats believe their experience in India will improve their future job prospects, compared with 43 per cent of expats across the Asia Pacific region.')

The above notwithstanding, when people announce to their family and friends that they are moving to India on work for a couple of years, they are, often times, not met with the reaction

---

* Quoted with permission from Expat Explorer: Achieving Ambitions Abroad, published in 2016 by HSBC Holdings plc.

they were looking for. The reasons are hardly surprising. Traditionally, an India move has been considered a 'hardship' posting, what with day-to-day living challenges like pollution, poor infrastructure and a paucity of good recreational options.

To put things in perspective, it's not just non-Indians who have reservations about moving to India. After spending nine years overseas, my Indian friends were amazed to hear that my family and I were heading back to India in 2012. They couldn't fathom why, after the comfort and ease of expatriate life in Asia, we wanted to come home – the operative word here being 'wanted'.

One reason for this amazement is the chaotic and complex nature of things in India.

But while living in India can be complicated, working in India doesn't have to be.

That said, the expatriate's expertise and talent coupled with the favourable market factors here do not automatically ensure success. Often, people who come here for a couple of years only skim the surface of what India is or has to offer, resisting greater interaction, involvement and understanding. The approach is: 'I'm here for three or four years. I don't need to look beyond the obvious. Let me focus on meeting my targets and whatever it takes to get there.'

While this approach is adopted by many, I found that the people who succeeded and enjoyed their stint in India all had one thing in common: they genuinely embraced India, the good and the bad. Needless to say, this translated into their professional success. It also gave a big upward boost to their post-India career trajectory.

However, this involves navigating some landmines. Tim Hume writes in a February 2012 article titled 'The secrets of doing business in India' for CNN: 'For foreign executives, doing business for the first time in India can be a bewildering experience. There's the new...but also the familiar.' The article goes on to quote a management professor at the University of Pennsylvania's Wharton School thus: 'You can get lulled into a false sense of security – "but for people dressing a little different and talking a little different, they are just like me". That's a completely false premise. There are all kinds of nuances in the culture, implicit cultural norms that we don't know about until we run afoul of them.'

Every culture has its underlying drivers of behaviours, values and beliefs and India is no exception. Embracing a culture entails going beneath the surface and figuring out the 'hows' and the 'whys'. And understanding these plays a significant part in success at one's job or assignment when working across cultures.

This book is a step in that direction. It aims to delineate the cultural nuances and complexities of working in professional organizations in India.

There is immense diversity in India – in terms of food, languages, celebrations, customs, dress and many more aspects. Across the country, people may talk, behave and think differently but, beneath the exterior, there are some values and beliefs that are common. These are explored and fleshed out here.

How India Works: Making Sense of a Complex Corporate Culture delves into the Indian's psyche and puts in perspective aspects like his hierarchical mindset and relationship- or people-focused approach. It attempts to answer questions like: What explains an Indian's readiness to come to work on holidays? Why does a person say 'yes' when in fact he means the opposite? It examines the implications of these nuances and how they get manifested at work.

It facilitates the Indian's understanding of how he is perceived through a multicultural lens. Nuances that are ingrained are brought to the fore, thereby enabling greater self-awareness. It highlights some areas which the Indian needs to work on in order to be more effective in an increasingly connected world. For instance, while communicating, sometimes less is more, and efforts matter but so do outcomes.

At the same time, this book also helps the non-Indian gain an understanding and an appreciation of a complex culture. For instance, to be cognizant of the importance of both hierarchy and relationships. And, while it could be frustrating, to appreciate the sentiment underlying the 'never-say-no' attitude. Importantly, it helps him navigate behaviours and mindsets such as these.

How India Works also aims to facilitate the transition of repatriated Indians, who have their share of living and working challenges as they try and reintegrate on coming 'home'. A dedicated chapter addresses their unique challenges of 'fitting in' professionally and personally and also enumerates the positives of being amongst one's people.

I have shared here my insights that reflect my varied experiences from the ringside of the corporate and training worlds, as someone who has worked in India and as an expat in Singapore and the Philippines over a period of nine years. These experiences have shaped my views and contributed to my writing. But the book is not limited to my views.

In writing this book, I have conducted sixty interviews with Indians and expatriates: twenty-four Indians (twelve knowledgeable experts in their fields and twelve who repatriated here after successful overseas stints) and thirty-six expatriates from countries such as the US, UK, Canada, Switzerland, France, the Netherlands, Belgium, Australia, New Zealand, Germany, Japan, South Korea, the Philippines, South Africa and Lebanon, all of whom are or were based in India at the time of writing this book. The interviewees were from diverse fields: senior executives at organizations in the areas of healthcare, information technology, financial and banking services, infrastructure, automobiles and scientific research. They also comprised members of the diplomatic corps, lawyers, international school educators, consultants and entrepreneurs. They shared their thoughts on working and living in India and spoke of their experiences – the positives and the challenges. They talked about how they interpreted and worked around cultural nuances and how they dealt with difficult circumstances.

Given that they have been here and done that, their experiences are extremely relevant for people in similar situations. As one of them said: 'Knowing the issues and problems is one half of solving them.'

Disclaimers

At the outset, there are a couple of disclaimers that I would like to state.

This is not a book on Indian culture per se. It is one only as far as it applies to the work culture in India. It is not a compilation of all nuances nor is it representative of every Indian, simply because India is too diverse.

How India Works focuses on the cultural drivers or values that are common to most Indians. Given the huge diversity, the nuances discussed here are those associated broadly with the urban, middle-class, graduate and above, white-collared Generation X (or older).

The perspectives and insights shared here are based broadly on my viewpoints and those of the people I have interviewed. They are not to be construed as principles or truths carved in stone, nor should they be seen as disrespectful of any culture.

They should be viewed for what they are – a means to facilitate a better understanding of working across different cultures.

All statements made, perspectives offered and opinions expressed are personal and not made in an official capacity. In instances where interviewees preferred not to be identified, I have changed their names when quoting them.

Lastly, here's an important caveat: This is not a book of recommendations, quick-fixes or instant solutions.

What one can expect from 'How India Works' is to get a feel and flavour of what to expect when working with Indians. The book contains some insights and experiences of people which the reader can leverage. With a balance of serious insights and humorous anecdotes, the Indian and the non-Indian gain an awareness of what works and what doesn't, and how to harness the strengths and work around the gaps.

But, finally, the reader will have to devise an approach or solution that would work best for him, keeping in mind his unique context, which will enable him to be successful in India.

Working and living in India is like driving on its roads – one hand on the horn and a foot on the brake, avoiding the potholes as you go along. This book helps one navigate the terrain and have a smoother, more fun ride!

1

Yes Boss

'So, John, how's it going so far?' Aditya asked his colleague, referring to his first couple of weeks in India as Chief Executive Officer of the bank. They were having lunch at one of Mumbai's oldest clubs.

John, taking a bite of his Chinese-only-in-name Schezwan Chicken, replied, 'You know, it's been quite good, actually. I haven't found an apartment yet that I have liked and that's taking a while to get sorted, but on the work front, it's been fairly smooth sailing. The office is great, people are friendly and professional. But I did notice one strange thing – people seemed to work very late, certainly much later than I have seen back home. You know that I have been working till about 8.30 or 9 p.m. most days since I am trying to familiarize myself with developments in the last few months in our business. But I noticed that I wasn't the only one working late; there were many people around. Is that the norm here?'

Aditya, who was the bank's Vice-President, laughed. He remarked, 'They work late because you work late. While people do work long hours in India, if there is a new boss, there is a *tendency, at least initially, to not leave office until he does. I wouldn't worry too much about it.'*

'But that doesn't make sense!' said John. 'I stay until late largely because my family is not here. I don't expect people at the office to hang around. They should leave when they are done and go home!'

Welcome to working in India!

This anecdote illustrates the hierarchy-ridden mindset prevalent in India. While hierarchy is an intrinsic aspect of organizations universally – and in some countries hierarchy is prevalent in the social context too – in India it is complex. Here, hierarchy is the silent operator that underlies or permeates many relationships.

It is most obvious between people who are separated by a clearly demarcated position – say, between the head of a department and a trainee, or a janitor and an office receptionist. But hierarchy is not restricted to differentiation in designations. It exists, in varying degrees, across the divisions of caste, age and gender.

There exists a mindset of mentally placing people in categories; this categorization determines the nature of behaviour meted out to them.

It's relative

At this point, I would like to refer to some data in the realm of intercultural research. Geert Hofstede,* a Dutch social

---

* Geert Hofstede, Gert Jan Hofstede, Michael Minkov, *Cultures and Organizations, Software of the Mind*, Third Revised Edition, McGrawHill 2010, ISBN 0-07-166418-1. © Geert Hofstede B.V., quoted with permission.

psychologist, developed a six-dimensional model explaining differences between national cultures. One of the dimensions called the Power Distance Index (PDI) may be a good reference to understand how different cultures are placed on the hierarchy spectrum. PDI is the extent to which the less powerful members of organizations and institutions accept and expect that power is distributed unequally. Simply put, countries that have high PDI scores have organizations and institutions that tend to be more hierarchical in nature, whereas in countries with low PDI scores, power is distributed more equally.

PDI scores of a few countries

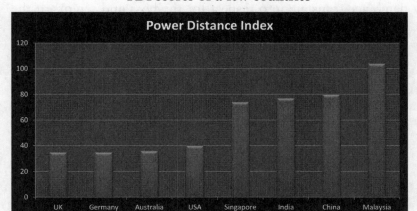

As can be seen from the graph, India's PDI score of 77 is on the higher side. While this study was done in the 1970s, these scores continue to be relevant as they give a broad idea of where India and other countries stand on certain parameters.

Hierarchy is not exclusive to India and is, in fact, relative. As Peter Clark, who was at the time of writing this book Chief Operating Officer for a large foreign company in India, points out:

Hierarchy is definitely present in India; it exists in other countries to a greater or lesser degree. Of the countries I have worked and lived in, Denmark is probably the least hierarchical, followed by the UK. Of the Asian countries, Japan is the most hierarchical. India is probably somewhere in between.

How hierarchy plays out at work

The value of respect for elders is ingrained in most Indians at an early age and is manifested in various ways like touching their feet or bowing to them for blessings. This intrinsic humility and deference translate into respect for the boss and seniors at the workplace.

That said, hierarchy, in the professional space in India, varies. Broadly speaking, in some Indian companies and public sector undertakings, the degree of hierarchy is high. It is toned down in Indian professional organizations, multinational companies and foreign banks, depending on the organizational culture, the values and mindset of the CEO and the senior leadership team.

Hari Sankaran, Vice Chairman of the IL&FS group in India, fleshes this out as he says: 'In government-owned public sector undertakings (PSU), the culture of hierarchy infuses the bureaucracy with a density that rivals black holes. In family-owned businesses, the culture of hierarchy allows family members plenipotentiary powers over staff, without reference to competence, experience, acumen, intelligence or outcomes. They belong to the family and that is sufficient. And then you have the professionally owned and managed corporates. They observe management principles, systems and processes and work cultures that are in sync with global practices. But they are still

Indian – which means that the culture of hierarchy will rear its head to varying degrees.'

Eric Labartette, former Managing Director of Metro One Operation, comments that 'in India, a boss is like God'. This may be a bit of an exaggeration, but there are vestiges of truth in this statement. And in organizations headed by foreigners, people look up to them more than they would an Indian boss.

On a slightly different but related note, also common to many Indians is the premium placed on fair skin. 'Fair is lovely' within India. The same degree of respect that is given to Caucasians is often not accorded to Asians or Africans.

A couple of expats I spoke with have experienced this. Stans Kleijnen, who is the Executive Director of the Netherlands Foreign Investment Agency for India, says, 'You just know that you are treated differently because of your skin colour. And it's often in little things like getting preferential treatment in a restaurant.'

Having established the broad contours, let's drill down a bit to understand some of the nuances better. This chapter explores some of the ways in which hierarchy impacts work in an organization. We also discuss how people have worked with and around the hierarchical mindset to be more effective.

At the outset, hierarchy in the workplace seems to operate on two levels. One is at the primary level of optics, where treatment is visibly different depending on where one is in the pecking order.

In an organization where I worked, coffee was served in bone china cups for the senior managers while those who were below a certain level drank coffee in simpler, less fancy mugs. An Asian expat, Kevin (name changed), observes: 'These are small things but you can feel them. For example, when you are out and you are ordering something, the most junior guy will be the one to coordinate.'

Big boss

How often has one seen a 'boss' getting out of his car while talking animatedly on his mobile phone, with his chauffeur opening his door and an assistant carrying his files? In India, if you are the boss, you need to be seen behaving like one.

Virginia Holmes, Director of Fat Mu, a premier make-up academy, says:

> When we are on set, being a Brit and accustomed to it, I would carry my make-up bags. And some of the guys on my team say to me, 'You cannot be seen carrying the bags, you're the boss!' I am, like, 'Don't be stupid,' because where I come from, everybody carries everything, you're a team. But here they push me forward with respect, take the bags from me, which is quite interesting because you have to be seen to be a boss! You get judged here.

It is a 'status' thing. As observed by an interviewee, 'The hierarchy is very important. My secretary Vinita has an assistant, Dev, the office boy. Vinita will not do the filing, the scanning or make the coffee because those are Dev's jobs. That doesn't happen anywhere else in the world!'

Scott (name changed), a senior executive at a multinational organization, offers an interesting perspective:

> We recently moved offices in Mumbai. My old office at the plant was like a fortress – a big reception area for my secretary, meeting room and my office. It was a very grand, very spacious corner office. When we moved to the new office, which is an open-plan office and much less imposing, my secretary really struggled.

In the old office, no one could see me or visit me; now in the new one, they can see me, and if they see that I'm in my office, somebody will just walk in – and they can just walk straight past her, which I don't mind. My approach is: 'If I'm there, come in.' But, for her, that was and still is a big issue because she feels that she's being undermined. She feels that she should be the gatekeeper! That's the dynamics of hierarchy coming into play with the office structure being changed!

Talk like the boss

At times, it's important to be assertive and talk like a boss as that's accepted and also expected. This is Virginia's viewpoint:

In India, loud and powerful = acceptable. I sometimes change my style in different situations. When I'm in the office, I'm quite easy-going; when I'm out, sometimes I am a bit more authoritative than I would like to be. If you're not that, they won't take you seriously. For example, our industry (cosmetics and make-up) is quite fun but it's very stressful as well. And sometimes, with my team, I will say, 'Guys, I need this done now, you've got to make it happen.' I say this firmly but without upsetting them at the same time.

The devi wears Prada

This particular tendency is more relevant for Indians who have repatriated after working overseas. The few that I spoke to mentioned that in their initial days and weeks back in India, the people they interacted with observed and reacted to the clothes and accessories they wore – in a sense 'checking them out'. This was not something they experienced as much when they were overseas; they may have been observed but no more or less than their colleagues.

Ashish Vijayakar, a senior officer at a foreign bank, puts it succinctly when he says, 'People don't react to you as a person. First, they react to your designation, to the car you drive, to the watch you have on, so it is obviously a lot more materialistic. These are a few things that hit you when you come back.'

I recall experiencing some of these behaviours when I moved back to India with my family. While it's not a big deal, it can be a bit annoying or strange because one is coming 'home' and does not expect to be seen through this lens.

These are a few areas where hierarchy is observed at a superficial level. But it can run deeper. It may translate into a person not empowering his subordinates sufficiently or questioning why an associate seems to enjoy certain perks that are commensurate with a higher position. These actions may be deliberate but, often, they may occur on a subconscious level on account of the inherent conditioning of the manager who has a hierarchical mindset.

So, moving from the external or superficial, let's look at a few areas where hierarchy makes a deeper impact:

Decision making

Hierarchy in the corporate environment exists everywhere, as it should. But a friend based overseas points out that although he works for a bureaucratic organization, as an employee he has the freedom to think of ideas and take decisions independently. And there is a high degree of inherent accountability.

Hierarchy in the Indian corporate set-up has a different connotation – and the difference is varied depending on the nature and culture of the organization.

Let's consider how decisions are taken. Broadly speaking, the tendency to push decisions higher up is more prevalent in organizations with a greater hierarchical culture. 'In professionally managed Indian companies or multinational corporations, as long as the teams are capable, they are empowered to take decisions,' Sangeeta (name changed), Human Resources Director of a large organization, remarked.

But this is not etched in stone. There are many cases of people not wanting to take decisions or pushing them higher up even in professional organizations. For instance, an expat at a foreign bank observes, 'When you are new, you want to gauge what your boss likes and how much he wants to be involved but I'm past that stage now and I still get shown drafts of emails before they are sent. My direct reports are keen to impress and keen to get things done. Sometimes I want them to be more empowered: take the decision and get on with it, but they want to refer back frequently.'

On a similar note, the head of a pharmaceutical organization shares that he is often consulted on things that the business unit heads have the authority to decide. 'They always bring decisions on people-related issues up to me,' he says.

What are the reasons for this?

This tendency is more pronounced at lower levels where traditionally employees weren't allowed to take decisions. Amit Agarwal, who moved to India as Vice-President and Country Leader with Thermo Fisher Scientific for a three-year assignment, says: 'When I got here, if I tried to enforce decision making at the levels that should be making those decisions, people struggled to do that, partly due to the culture and partly because we had not empowered them. It's a chicken-and-egg situation.'

Sven De Wachter, Director of Wachter Oriental, says, 'I see many cases where people push decisions up, but I also see as many cases where Indians take decisions when you empower them and give them the chance to take responsibility. Maybe 50 per cent do not want to take decisions because they were never allowed and were never taught to take decisions.'

These behaviours also stem from the mindset that 'the boss always knows best'. Kevin shares:

> I asked my team, 'Why don't you guys make a decision, why do you have to elevate it?' One of the guys told me, 'You are the boss! You are the one supposed to be making the decisions. We look up to you to make decisions.'

In India, initiative is often demonstrated not as much in finding the solution but in identifying the problem! There is a boss culture rather than a team culture; people will look up to the boss to find the solution.

Madhav Kalyan, MD and CEO, JPMorgan Chase Bank N.A., India, points out, 'If there is a problem, you won't find too many people coming up with solutions saying, "These are the three things I am thinking of: let's debate and pick what's the best." They come to you and say, "I have this problem, now help me deal with it. And they will look to you for a solution. So I keep telling them, "A leader is not an oracle who can just give solutions! Let's think through or come up with a few alternatives." Otherwise they are happy to come and dump a problem.'

An expat, who has worked and lived in four continents, says succinctly: 'It's a challenge here because people expect you, as the boss, to have the knowledge, the experience and the answers! You must have them all – they expect that of you!'

Related to this observation, Rajesh (name changed), Managing Director of a large multinational organization, remarks, 'Given the calibre of the people I work with, while I don't have to micromanage, you still have to get involved in a lot of things. They put you in the loop and, at senior levels, everybody will expect you to know the smallest detail!'

On the flip side, a boss who is used to giving solutions and instructions may find it difficult to accept that someone else can come up with a solution. And if that someone else is a manager two levels below or an administrative assistant, one can only imagine how that will pan out!

How does one work around this?

With regard to encouraging colleagues to come up with solutions, here's an example of how an expat adapted his communication style to be more effective, given the hierarchy:

You ask more questions, you don't give much information up front, you stay back. You need to engage your team in a way that they become comfortable with the subject. You try and get them to start talking and, once they start, Indians can talk! And sometimes what I do is I just keep quiet when there are a couple of people, and that silence will make somebody uncomfortable and he will start talking. It's not easy. You ask one person, 'How would you solve it?' or 'What do you think of it?' And ask this same question to the next person and so on. They are then forced to think about the problem and they may come up with a damn good solution!

As regards facilitating decisions being made at lower levels, the boss plays a critical role. He can encourage decision making by way of effective delegation and empower his subordinates. He could communicate the nature of decisions that employees can and should take; they should only seek his approval when it's necessary.

Eric Labartette explains how he worked around this: 'In the beginning, we drafted job descriptions saying, "This is your responsibility, you have to take responsibility for these things." In the beginning, every ten minutes my phone would ring and my colleagues would ask me what to do. I would say to them that they are competent enough. Now they take decisions within certain limits. Beyond those limits, they have to call me.'

Regular on-the-job mentoring and coaching help to manage gaps and to set expectations up front. Eventually, and most importantly, the leader has to walk the talk. In India, one sees examples of leaders who talk of empowering their subordinates but when the latter take decisions that don't pan out well, they don't always support them. To create an effective culture of decision making, bosses have to stand by decisions taken by their juniors or peers.

This is illustrated by Hari Sankaran: 'I often advise my colleagues to transfer the blame upwards if things go wrong and push credit downwards if things go right. I do not know how well it has worked in actual practice, but it does seem to have built a more collegial, transparent and professional work environment.'

As an interviewee tells his team: 'Listen guys, we are not going to penalize each other for whatever mistakes we make. We'll just move on and learn from them.'

Communicating at work

An Indian, who repatriated, puts it well when he says: 'When you come to India, you get a new last name, because everybody now calls you by your name followed by "Sir"!' While this practice is more prevalent in public sector or family-owned companies (where Hindi words like 'Saheb' or the suffix 'ji' are added to denote respect), it's less common within professional organizations but it depends on the leader and the organizational culture. In general, people aren't comfortable calling their bosses or seniors by first names.

It is important for the non-Indian to be cognizant of the way the hierarchical set-up works: accept it and adapt. Just as he is given respect, he too needs to be appropriately respectful of senior people within and outside the organization.

Going beyond how people address each other, let's examine some of the ways in which hierarchy impacts communication at work, especially with one's boss. Rajan Khorana, former Director at a large US-based financial institution, narrates this incident that occurred when he was working in the US:

'I will do anything that my boss says' seems to be the mantra for Indians, generally speaking. But they take it to the next level where cooperation between teams is not that good because of different managers coordinating, and they are often running in different directions. For example, when I was in the US, we were trying to get a job done from another team within our company. Specifically, we were seeking help from a developer named Alok (name changed) who was Indian and based in the US. We asked Alok how long the task was going to take. He said it would take him three weeks to do it. This was absolutely unacceptable from a timeline point of view. So we tried to understand why it was going to take that long. That didn't work, so we checked with his manager if we could put more people on the task to get it done on time. The manager said, 'Don't worry, I'll get it done,' and then he spoke with Alok. He asked him how long it would take to do the job. Alok said, 'I can get it done in three days.' We were, like: 'What the hell just happened here?!'

The above incident illustrates how hierarchy and personal connect (discussed in the next chapter) impact not only communication but also implementation. An interesting thing to note is that hierarchy is prevalent not only amongst Indians who are based in India, but also those who are based overseas. Some traits are ingrained.

This is another example, as narrated by an expat, of how Indian colleagues communicate with their boss, in this case a foreigner:

My previous boss hosted dinner parties where he would always use the same caterer. I didn't particularly like the food at his parties, nor did the local Indian staff. When I asked them, 'Have you ever told him?' they said, 'Yes, we've told him.' Later, when I checked with my boss, he said, 'People have never told me. I wish they had told me.' But he probably couldn't hear it because they weren't explicit enough as they didn't want to insult him. So, for three years my boss had unknowingly served terrible food at his functions. He wouldn't eat it himself because he didn't like Indian food and nobody ever *really* told him!

As seen in the example above, the boss may not 'get' the message from his colleagues since it may be cloaked by restraint and politeness. People may be hesitant to share what they really think. Given this reticence, this is Scott's take on how he adapted his behaviour to be more effective:

In the beginning I would ask people if they agreed with me. But I would not get to know what they really thought. So then I rephrased my question and started asking: 'What do you think? How would you do it? If you were in my position, what would you do?' So I don't get directly into the subject but rather go around and get their opinions in another way. Because, if you say, 'This is what I have done, is this okay?' they'll say, 'Yes, it's okay, it's great.' So you've got to try other ways of finding out what they think.

Related to the above, Kevin observes, 'The burden is on me, as the boss':

Indians express their views and articulate them well. But I don't think they will give you negative feedback unless you seek it. They will think, 'If I say this to my boss, how will he take it?' So the burden is on me to actually find that out — create an environment where my subordinate can openly express his view and at the same time feel that he is doing me a favour! But that only happens after a period of time when you get to know him and he starts feeling comfortable. And sometimes you can do it indirectly also by making a joke out of it.

Questioning or challenging the boss

In the Indian context, one has grown up learning to accept (to an extent) what parents and teachers say and not challenge them or debate with them. This mindset gets carried over to the workplace in varying degrees. Employees at lower levels are reluctant to question or challenge the boss but this seldom happens even amongst senior employees. This reticence could be more pronounced in the case of a non-Indian boss.

A couple of people I interviewed attributed this to wanting to be on the good side of the boss. So, if they challenge the boss, they feel that it may negatively impact business and their careers. The line between the professional and the personal is a bit blurred.

An interviewee, who headed a business in India, says, 'In the organization, you want somebody to challenge your thinking. But it doesn't happen enough. I don't find Indians aggressive or argumentative. I don't find many examples of pushing back. That bothers me. You need to tell me, "That's not a good idea."'

On the other hand, some Indians I spoke to felt that it was routine to get asked questions and to be challenged. Mukesh (name changed), a senior executive with a large American organization, observes, 'Indians are more disposed to speaking their minds freely than people in other Asian countries. The level of questioning or scrutiny for people in senior positions is more intense in India than in other places where people have questions but will be more reluctant to ask. This should not be a surprise. Look at what's happening in Indian politics. Where else do you see such a vibrant, argumentative democracy anywhere in Asia? So something like that is also happening in our corporate environment.'

Ashish Vijayakar has a similar view: 'It's far more likely that people will disagree or challenge you here than in the markets that I have worked in.'

In the multinational corporation (MNC) framework, it is possible to strike the right balance between challenge and support. Sangeeta says that in her organization, an MNC, it is normal to challenge and be challenged. 'Culturally, we, as HR managers, encourage this but it also depends on the business leaders and what they want as the culture.'

However, notwithstanding the above, hierarchy, even in an MNC, seems to be alive and kicking. This is an incident narrated by an expat:

> We have a number of independent directors along with whom I participate in the audit committee meetings, remuneration committee meetings and so on. Our chairman doesn't participate in the audit committee meetings. I attend these along with the directors and later the chairman joins us and that's when I see how the directors' behaviour changes. They are very vocal inside the audit committee, but once the chairman comes in, it's not the same. Their body language becomes more deferential, they don't challenge as much, they show more respect, nod more and it is the chairman who asks questions and challenges them. This is not to say that this does not happen elsewhere in the world, but it's not as evident as it is here. The surprising thing is that these are very senior people, who are sixty or seventy years old, with years and years of experience. More importantly, it's also noteworthy because they are all independent directors; they are not really answerable to anybody.

So, even in multinational organizations, hierarchy is manifested in different ways and degrees.

Kanchana TK, Director General, Organization of Pharmaceutical Producers of India (OPPI), shares an interesting viewpoint: 'In meetings, I've observed if there are senior people, everyone agrees; no one disagrees in that group. It's not a heterogeneous group, so where are you going to get a different opinion?'

There does not seem to be much appreciation and respect for diversity of thinking. This view is corroborated by Jeetu Panjabi, part of the senior management at a large global financial company in India, who worked overseas for eight years before repatriating: 'Overseas, it is a mix of people from different cultures – Japanese, Chinese, Korean, German, Singaporean, American, etc. In India, everyone is very "Indian". Their thinking is very similar, and it lacks a global or different perspective.'

I asked several people how they tried to encourage a more open and transparent culture. The people I spoke with, many of whom helm large organizations, said that they would encourage their top teams and people below to express their concerns. The general consensus was that, with time and continuous and repeated encouragement from the people at the top, things change. But it's usually only the senior team that begins to challenge and question; it seldom percolates to the lower levels.

As Joe King, the former head of Audi, India, says:

> The culture is of not challenging the status quo. I have tried to bring this in with my direct reports but have not been very successful down the line.

When I asked an expat if people were open and frank with him, he replied, 'Not initially, I think it evolved. Those who are younger or more junior tend to keep to themselves at first, so you need to stimulate them without offending them or rocking the boat.'

What is imperative for a culture of openness is to have a good rapport or trust in place. This is discussed at length in the next chapter.

Discussion and sharing of views

It's important to note here that while there may not be much open challenging or disagreement, there is a good amount of discussion and sharing of views in organizations.

Pranav (name changed), a senior banking professional, says, 'I think over the years what a lot of multinational companies have been doing is that they promote open dissent and open voicing of views. There is no sycophancy at all. And in a country like ours, with demographics like ours, if everybody has a view, everybody has a view! So if you have to get everybody on the same page, it's challenging and it takes a lot more effort.' This is put in perspective by a European on his second stint in India:

If I compare with the Asian country where I was before moving to India, it's different here in the way hierarchy is executed. When you take Germany for comparison, there's a lot of questioning. So, you might have a decision at the top management level and a lot of people may feel that it's not the right decision, and there's a lot of talk about it. In the Asian country, it was the absolute other side. The boss says something and they all do it. There is no questioning of that. It might be a completely wrong decision to go left instead of right, but everyone goes left because the boss has told so.

In India it's a nice in-between.

So if people feel that it's not the best decision, there will be discussion around it, but at the end of the day it's: 'Let's do it, let's get it done.' In India, there's definitely more listening, discussion, feedback than what you would see in an East Asian country, which is much more hierarchical. And especially for a foreigner in a management/leadership role, the feedback from your staff, if you don't know the country, if you don't know the marketplace, is crucial. In India, there is actually a nice balance.

A British expat, Simon (name changed), has a similar view. He says that while he had expected more challenge and confrontation because of his earlier experience of working with Indians, one definitely gets more debate and critique here than in many Asian countries. 'It's pretty similar to the West in that sense.'

It's relevant to mention here that the younger generation is driven differently in this respect. As Shanti Mohan, co-founder and CEO, LetsVenture, says, 'The younger generation today will question authority. If you are able to convince them, they will respect you. They are not blind followers.'

When hierarchy can be effective

We've discussed above some aspects and fallouts of a hierarchical mindset that may not be entirely ideal or desirable from an organizational viewpoint. That said, it's relevant to state here that hierarchy can be beneficial and is, in fact, essential to the smooth and efficient functioning in organizations.

Hari puts this in perspective: 'Hierarchies are a very necessary condition for efficient implementation. Creativity, innovation and decision making have their place. The culture of hierarchy, if used appropriately, allows a ruthless focus on efficiency, keeping the team on track though implementation, and cutting to the chase as required.'

Sateen Bailur, Senior Manager at a large foreign bank, remarks: 'It wasn't decisions that were pushed up as much as disagreements. If there was disagreement between two people, they would not be able to deal with it in a mature fashion, so I had to step in and say, "Hey, just do this."'

The point is to use one's position as a leader to channelize discussions productively. And in another's words, 'Sometimes you just have to put your foot down and say this is the way to do it.'

Not just in meetings but in day-to-day working too, the hierarchical mindset can be effective. An expat made this comment: 'On the positive side, in terms of managing, the hierarchy makes it very easy because generally there's a set pecking order. Not that it isn't so in the West, but here it's much more defined and that can be advantageous when you are managing staff and trying to get things done. You can issue directives and that makes your life easier. I've heard other foreign managers say that it's easier to manage staff in India than it would be back in my home country.'

To this I would say, yes, hierarchy is effective but a leader or boss who issues clinical instructions, dictates directives and demands tasks to be carried out will be heard and obeyed – not necessarily respected or liked. Because he is the boss, people will follow what he says but a transactional approach works only to a point. What is needed to be effective in the longer term on a sustainable basis is an approach where the leader connects with his people. A boss has to strike a balance between being authoritative and also caring and concerned.

This is where the relationship-centred approach comes in, which is addressed in the relevant chapter.

Titles matter

An HR director narrates this:

> This high-potential manager once came up to me and said, 'I am bored of doing this; I need to do something different.' I asked her what she would like to do; she had identified a few jobs that she could do but they weren't opening up for a while. After much hemming and hawing, she came to the point and asked me: 'Which job can I do so that I get a change of title?'

Due to social pressures or expectations, upward mobility is perceived by a change in job titles. If one is in the same position for more than two years, that person may be perceived by his peers and family as not 'growing' or, worse, stagnating.

Madhav remarks, 'Typically, an Indian organization has around fifteen levels between the top and entry-level management graduates. A person expects a change in title every two years; so he needs those fifteen stairs to climb.'

Eric gives an interesting example of how they worked around this internally:

> We have few titles because we are a flat organization. People were not comfortable with it since after three to four years, they still had the same title. Even if I give a person a 10 per cent increment every year, he still wants to leave because he does not have a good title. Finally, we created some new titles. For example, earlier we had only 'Manager' but now we have Assistant Manager, Manager and Senior Manager. Interestingly, all three designations have the same salary!

Titles matter not just in India but everywhere. Universally, people want recognition and they give importance to titles. But in India, the degree to which they matter is different. India is an ascriptive society where status is accorded on the basis of one's designation and corresponding position in society. As titles reflect this position, they matter. Whether it's clients or bureaucrats, government or regulatory officials, they often want to meet the seniormost people in an organization. And even though these senior people may not be the most knowledgeable or well-versed in the facts of the case, it is an illustration of their organization's commitment when they attend these meetings.

And people want these titles on their visiting cards, which often, for similar reasons, also display one's qualifications. An expat who joined an MNC in Mumbai found that people regarded him initially with a degree of scepticism. This may have been because he was relatively young and didn't have much experience despite assuming a senior position. But the minute they learned that he had earned his postgraduate degree from Harvard University in the US, he was viewed differently.

Here is an example of how a change in title made a difference:

> Our sales representatives were known as Business Developers. We implemented a transformational project; one of the outcomes of which was that we changed the titles of the sales representatives to Business Managers. A few weeks later, we received a video clip from one sales representative. This is what he said: 'Dear sirs, because of my change in title, I got married. Until now, nobody wanted to get married to me because I was a business developer, now I am a manager! The company has given wings to my dreams. Thank you!'

Not going outside the box

Often it is seen that people do as they are told and do not step beyond their designated functions or roles. This could be because they lack the confidence and are afraid of making mistakes. Another factor could be that since organizations and departments are frequently staffed with high numbers of employees, tasks are fragmented, with each person doing his delineated bit. This arrangement does not lend itself to people extending themselves to go beyond the tasks they are responsible for. It's like saying: 'This is my job. I will only do "this"; anything outside of "this" is your job.'

This is more pronounced at lower levels and in administrative roles but is seen elsewhere too. James (name changed), an executive at a multinational healthcare company, had this observation of more senior managers: 'A challenge is getting cross-functional teams to go beyond their little boxes, and it is accentuated by hierarchy.'

Here's a perceptive observation shared by Craig Johnson, head of the American School of Bombay: 'Sometimes I think this tendency in some Indians to stay within their "boxes" has to do with their deep belief in reincarnation. As if this is the life assigned to a certain role, and so that's what they will be. They do not go out of their way to show their potential beyond that assignment. But you also find staff, especially Indian millennials, who think they can literally do anything. They think they can go from being a secretary to running the school in ten years.'

Conclusion

In conclusion, here are some experiences and perspectives on how people have worked with and around hierarchy in India to be more effective.

These are Simon's insights regarding connecting with people across levels:

> I make a point of engaging with everyone in my organization — whether it's the security man or a peer — and I don't think that happens much. Clearly, parts of society here are very hierarchical. You smile at people, you talk to them, you ask them how they are. Some people have looked surprised and remained very formal. People won't take the first step to break the hierarchy, but if you do, they will open up.

Susanne Cox, a senior HR manager currently on assignment in an Indian petrochemicals organization, shares her learnings and experience:

The importance of hierarchy here has been a very big learning for me. At times I can see that people have got some brilliant ideas, you can see from their body language that they might disagree with what's being said, but they don't voice it because they are dealing with someone more senior. There's a desire to change things culturally at my organization, empower people more and give them the courage to stand up and say, 'I disagree,' or, 'I've got a great idea, how about we do it this way?' But the overriding cultural importance of hierarchy can prevent that sometimes.

I've had to be more mindful of it, I've had to check my language and how I approach people. An example would be, if I know somebody well, who may be someone more senior to me, I wouldn't hesitate to go and see them. If they were in their office and even if the door were closed, I would knock and stick my head in and say, 'Do you have five minutes?' Here, I did it a couple of times and then found out that if it was someone senior, you don't do that. You go through their secretary or ask if they are free and take an appointment. So I realized I needed to change my behaviour to adapt to a different culture. Otherwise I might not get respect from that individual; worse still, I might be offending them.

Craig shares a great example of working with and around the hierarchy:

We used to be a school on a single campus and, a few years ago, we decided to have two campuses. So we bought flat land and initiated the process of actually building a new school on the second campus. In the course of one year, we designed the building, we built the building and we moved into the building. At the same time, we gutted the existing building and reconfigured it. And no one in India could believe we did this in one year!

My team and I would be on site going from one floor to the next, nudging the work along. At the start of the project, when we would see the workers sitting and not doing anything, we would walk over and get them to start working again. Our being there instead of sitting in an office far away changed the culture of work on the site.

The point is we broke through all hierarchies. Basically we would eat together, we would have biryani on Fridays, the workers' kids would come and play in the swimming pool. Some workers had elderly parents, whom we brought in from Bihar; we put them up in an inexpensive hotel here so they didn't have to worry about their families.

Hierarchy being left alone is a disaster. But if you engage with it and provide professional development, encourage collaboration and related inputs, people will rise to the occasion.

As mentioned earlier, humility is a virtue in India, one that is often manifested in varying degrees of deference. Non-Indians often perceive the respectful, non-confrontational Indian as lacking in aggression. And while that may be true in some cases, this perception is not always accurate. Underneath that reticent and conformist exterior is often an independent streak and a determination to make things happen. The Indian is often understated, yet aggressive and driven in his own way.

As discussed earlier, hierarchy is relative. A Senior Director, of Japanese origin, observes of Indian offices: 'It is a comfortable working atmosphere, with people approaching each other easily irrespective of positions. In Japan, the adherence to hierarchy is much more.' While extreme manifestations of the hierarchical mindset are less prevalent today, especially amongst the younger generation, hierarchy exists in India in varying degrees, shapes and forms. One should accept it, work with or around it.

In general, a polite but firm style works well. People want a boss to be nice but also someone who knows what he wants and is not afraid to seek (or demand) it. This is especially relevant for the Indian repatriate, as he may adopt a less hierarchical and friendly approach, given that he is now amongst his 'own' people.

Jeetu Panjabi, on his return to India, realized this and adapted his behaviour. He says, 'I figured that in India when you communicate with a power quotient, it ensures that people take instructions seriously. In Singapore, where I lived for eight years, things are black and white. Here, a lot of things are grey. I would feel like: remove the grey, cut out the chaff and give it to me as it is. I would often be firmer and tougher than I would have been elsewhere.'

Rajan Khorana sums it up well: 'It's how you implement, adapt and make use of hierarchy rather than trying to remove it, because removing it is a big shift. How do you work with it to your advantage rather than abolish it? Hierarchy puts power at the top. How do you reverse it? Keep the hierarchy as it is and start empowering people under you. So you leave the system unchanged but you change the mindset. Let people make decisions and support them as they make mistakes and have failures. Communicate your values and create an open, inclusive culture. If you, sitting at the top, are going to question everything, you are promoting hierarchy.'

As a leader, one is in a good position to influence the organizational culture and way of working. The hierarchical approach is a given, but if one has the time, persistence and perseverance, one can mould people to ultimately take on ownership at a higher level than they are used to.

2

The Art of Managing the Heart

When I moved back to India some years ago, I was looking for a place where I could buy vegetables and fruits – a shop that was clean, fresh and had a wide range of products, something similar to our shopping experience overseas. The Nature's Basket outlet near my house seemed like a good option. Initially, when I would go there, the staff were polite, would answer my queries and help me with finding some of the produce I needed. Now that I have become a regular customer, the minute they see me, they smile, get me a cart and a trolley, and help me with the bags to get the vegetables weighed.

What's more is that they share useful nuggets like, 'No madam, don't take these tomatoes. I will get you from the stock that's just arrived', or 'The best time to get surti palak is after 2.30 p.m. Send your driver then.' At times, while billing, if the cashier thinks that the melon I have chosen (that looks fine from the outside) seems a bit overripe, he sends his colleague to get me a new one. I was recently advised when I was looking for minced mutton that a particular brand was great but I shouldn't buy the same for whole mutton as it wasn't tender enough.

Needless to say that this personalized attention makes for a fulfilling shopping experience – one that I didn't have when we were overseas. It probably makes a difference that I am of the same nationality as the staff in this shop, but I see them extending this service to non-Indians too. On the flip side, not every Indian gets this service. They help not just because they are expected to but because they genuinely want to. It seems to me that a big part of the reason why the salespersons go beyond 'their job' is the 'connect' I have with them.

This personal connect permeates and impacts social, personal and professional areas in India. But doesn't that apply universally? Yes. Good business relationships matter everywhere, not just in India or Asia. An interviewee, Shashi (name changed), an executive at a financial institution, who recently returned to India after some years in New York, feels that the way he connects with clients is the same whether he is in India or the US. He says, 'As I am in sales, I would have "relationship-based" introductions with clients in India as well as in New York. In some cases, cold calling worked there and it works here. But by and large, I don't see it as very different in either place.'

If client interface is part of the job, as it is in the instance above, connecting with the client is important irrespective of where one is based. But in India, there is often a need to connect even if this is not the case. For example, within the organization, while the boss is accepted and respected because he is (first and foremost) the boss, that's not enough. People need to feel that sense of connect; trust is an important part of the workplace dynamics. And while relationships are important universally, the degree to which they matter in India is different.

This chapter examines and elaborates on the various ways in which personal connections impact work in India. It fleshes out characteristics of the friendly (and at times over-friendly) Indian and discusses some ways to build trust and rapport.

The family factor

Let's begin with where relationships originate. The seeds of the Indian's attitude to building relationships and creating trust are, in all probability, sown at home. Chances are, if you ask Indians what is the thing of most value to him or her, seven out of ten will say 'family'.

An illustration of this can be the way a typical interview for an entry-level or field position goes, as narrated by Sangeeta, who is in the HR space:

> Chetan, the HR Director, greets Ravikant, who is applying for the position of a sales representative, and says: 'Tell me a bit about yourself.' Ravikant says, 'Sir, my name is Ravikant Kumar. I am from Indore. I have a family of five people. My father works as a maths teacher in a school, my mother is a housewife. My brother is working in an engineering company. My sister is in the twelfth standard. I did my BCom and then joined such-and-such company. I have worked there for four years.'

According to Sangeeta, the above is illustrative of how people in smaller cities and towns typically respond when asked about themselves – they talk about their families. As an aside, it's worth noting that questions about the family are commonly asked in India in job interviews. Notwithstanding the fact that joint families are fewer today and more people live in nuclear set-ups, the extended family still plays a fairly big role. One's relationships and networks form an important source of support from childhood. So, in a sense, it seems natural for this tendency to connect and belong to get carried over to the workplace.

Ali Sleiman, former General Manager of a multinational pharmaceutical organization in India, puts it succinctly: 'In Lebanon, family values and structure are very strong, but Indians probably take it a step further because it's very common to see three generations of a family living in the same house.'

So, for an average Indian, family connections are very important. Can it then be inferred that Indians are group-oriented and collectivists? Shanti says, 'For us it's about "what is our collective calling?" We don't give much priority to ourselves. The sense of self and "I" is not very strong in India.' One has seen instances of how one's personal goals are often sacrificed or put on hold in the greater interest of the family. But while Indians could be termed 'group-oriented', the 'group' is a small one, usually the immediate family or peer groups. In the Indian context, there is a duality – people are contextual in how they adapt. In the social context, people are collective-oriented, but in terms of work, they are more individualistic. Susanne makes a perceptive observation: 'There's a really competitive element here, and while I have seen some brilliant examples of teamwork, my experience is that when it comes to what people are delivering and how they are performing, it's often about the individual.'

This is elaborated upon in an article in the *Ivey Business Journal* issue of March/April 2005 by Rajesh Kumar, Associate Professor of International Business at the Aarhus School of Business, Denmark. Titled 'Negotiating with the complex, imaginative Indian', it states that the simultaneous presence of individualism and collectivism distinguishes the Indian manager not only from his North American counterpart but also from his East Asian peer who is unquestioningly collectivist in his or her orientation. The article goes on to state that Indians are, on the whole, more Western than Eastern in their way of thinking, implying thereby that they can behave either in an individualistic or in a collectivist manner, depending on the situation.

Now let's examine how the accent on relationships impacts behaviour at work. This is Kanchana's perspective, which is a good starting point:

> I think we indulge people because of our social structures. It's very 'community'-focused; it's cultural. I've seen managers who come in, do the small talk, build relationships and that works for them. Others who are more transactional, they talk about the work, do the work and go home. The one who chats is perceived to be a better leader. So, perceptions are driven by how relationship-driven you are and not by the effectiveness of the job.
>
> Working in India, I often get feedback that I'm very effective but I need to be more relationship-driven. I recognize that it's a cultural nuance and I have often tried to incorporate the style in small doses.

One can see from the above the importance of building relationships at work in India. Let's consider some nuances of the relationship- or people-oriented approach in India.

Fragile – handle with care

Saving face is important across cultures and India is no exception. And just as Indians are conscious of causing loss of face to others, they are equally concerned about losing face themselves. The quintessential Indian phrase, 'Log kya kahenge?', or 'What will people say?', underlines outward behaviours and conduct to some extent. People are conscious of what their neighbours, relatives and their laundry man think of them – and not necessarily in that order! Indians are a sensitive lot, concerned about their reputation and how they are perceived. Given the hierarchical mindset, they expect to be accorded respect commensurate with their position and status in society.

This thinking, when carried over to the workplace, results in people being worried or afraid of offending their boss and peers, whether it's by taking 'wrong' decisions or saying the politically incorrect thing. This mindset may be, in part, due to the value of ahimsa, which means 'cause no injury'. This is articulated in the book *Cultural DNA: The Psychology of Globalization*, whose author Gurnek Bains makes the point that the concept of ahimsa influences Indian attitudes in areas like sport, negotiations and while conducting business.

People care about how bad news is communicated; difficult conversations can take longer here than elsewhere. This is highlighted by Hari:

At heart, Indians are very sociable and tend to personalize relationships. For this reason, they don't like to deliver bad news or say 'no'. And if they have to, they would take an inordinate amount of time.

I discovered this early in my working life, when we were closing an operation and had to retrench senior staff. On reviewing the progress, I found that very little had been done although days had been spent in discussion. When confronted, the head of the unit, Pramod (name changed), finally admitted his difficulty in communicating the decision. The next morning, we invited the people concerned and explained the circumstances that the company was facing, the decisions that were being taken, and the separation package. All in all, fifteen minutes.

After the meeting, Pramod turned to me and said that he saw these folks as part of his family and found it very difficult to be clinical and dispassionate. He confided that he had actually brought packed lunch, anticipating that the meeting might last the whole day!

The softer, humane side is displayed in many situations, but a common one is when a person falls critically ill or meets with an accident and is hospitalized. That his family members will visit him is of course a given but often so will his colleagues.

I recall, many years ago when we were overseas, my husband had undergone a surgery and was hospitalized for a few weeks. I received one call and some text messages from his colleagues and that was it. I remember thinking it would have been nice to have a bit more emotional support. Of course, the experience I had whilst overseas is not the norm and it depends on the circumstances and people, but in India the emotional support rendered in times like these is pretty much a given. Virginia says:

I think the people have so much soul here. When I am on set here, there is great camaraderie. In India, people care about people. In a Western culture, they might say, 'Let's work through lunch,' but here you stop for lunch. There's much more of sensitiveness; it's having an old culture.

Business is personal

In India, business is personal; Indians need to feel they can trust the people they are doing business with. The process of building trust could be spread out over months, weeks or even hours; at a lunch, people could chat about other topics before getting into the business end of things.

As Madhav says: 'It's a culture of trust building, so it's not very transaction-oriented, which is why you have this dropping in for coffee and having a conversation. It's personality-driven, so if you hit it off as a personality, the solution will follow, the business will follow.'

This is not unique to India, but it is more pronounced here than in some other places. An interviewee points out, 'When you are comfortable with someone, you would rather go back to that person, and rely on that "trust" factor and the mental dependency of that relationship, which may well outweigh going to a third party, a stranger. This is true of emerging-market personalities. I would say it's probably the same with Mexicans or Brazilians or South Americans or Italians. So it's not necessarily only Indians. But yes, Indians do like EQ in their relationships.'

On a related note, it is not often that one sees deeply embedded and robust processes that are in place; rather, it is the individual or the few people who make things work. So work is more individual-dependent and, consequently, relationship-dependent.

However, the role that personal connections and relationships play cannot be generalized and depends on organizations, leadership and the organizational culture. In more professional organizations, it may, in fact, be transactional and very business-like due to changing standards, focus on professionalism and competition.

Here's a perspective from Pranav, part of senior management at a multinational bank:

In deal making, do relationships matter? Yes. But today, it being a transparent and competitive world, besides the relationship, you have to be competitive. Relationships give you that competitive edge. For example, a relationship may send you a feeler that yours may not be the best quote or deal. Or you may get the right to quote the last bid. For instance, 'I know you, I want to deal with you, but I've got a price of X. If you can match it, the deal is yours.' So that is what a relationship can get you.

The relationship process is not unique to India, but abroad it's more scientific. If you have a relationship and you're not getting enough deals, they question the relationship. In India, nobody questions relationships yet. Abroad they a) value relationships better and b) they are able to monetize relationships better. In India, the relationship is taken for granted by both parties.

Regarding hiring people, in professional Indian organizations and MNCs, relationships will not get you the job. Competence is the key criterion. If a good friend of mine applies for a job, a relationship will get someone to meet him seriously. After that his ability will be assessed. And if all things are equal, he is known to me, he's a better fit.

Meritocracy is of prime importance today. It's about having the basics or the ABCs – A (ability), B (break) and C (career). If you don't have the Ability, you're not going to get the Break and if you don't get the Break you're not going to have that Career.

Impacts implementation

Knowing the right person helps. This was especially true in the earlier days of the licence-permit raj, when red tape and bureaucracy slowed things down considerably unless one had a good equation with the person concerned. While India has come a long way since then, to some extent even in regular day-to-day functioning, knowing the 'right' person still plays a part.

The personal connect helps in getting work done. The reader would recall the anecdote in the previous chapter about Alok telling his boss that he would complete a task in three days, and not three weeks like he had mentioned to another manager. Alok's boss is able to get this commitment from him because of not just his position as a boss but also their working relationship.

An emotional connect can create greater buy-in and ownership among employees. While this is probably true universally, Indians perhaps respond to it better because of their strong relationship orientation. In this regard, Peter shares his insights below:

> I do feel that in India the hearts and minds are important. You have to take people on a bit of an emotional journey with you rather than saying, 'I am the boss. I want you to do this by this day. Go and do it.' There's a little more of an emotional connection needed in terms of, 'I want you to do this but here's why.' 'Here's why I think this is a good thing for us to do, and when you've done it, it will be great and you'll feel really good about it and everyone will appreciate it.' And to support this, yes, I use goals and targets. But I try and personalize it as much as I can.
>
> If I say, 'I am the boss, just do it,' what I'll get is people saying, 'Yes,' and then not doing it. When you can motivate them with a sense of achievement, you will get much better output. Indians value being valued. When they are given the background, when the bigger picture and the reasons for doing something are shared with them and they are trusted to do their best, they rise to the occasion.

On a similar note, Craig says, 'With people, what I've often been very successful doing is painting a picture of what you are building. When the labourers were moving bricks to build the

new school, we brought them in and showed them plans of the
school and videos of the kids. We told them, "You're building
the most important school in India," and their whole work ethic
just went up!'

Fosters loyalty

How the personal connect fosters loyalty is highlighted well
in this chat I had with Nick Kilstein and Chloe Kannan,
international school teachers, regarding their equations with the
local school staff. Nick said: 'Chloe and I are friends with them;
we treat them as equals. And we noticed that we receive special
treatment from the staff. In a Western sense, that's unfair, but I
think in an Indian sense, it's like: "Nick and Chloe take time to
make a relationship with us, so of course I am going to do more
for them." The sense of loyalty, I think, is what trumps all else.'

This is another instance, shared by Rajan, of how relationships
impact working in India. 'In India, people at the lower levels can
get paid at least 10 per cent more than what they are being
currently paid, so why should a person not leave their job? It's
almost like you have to make sure that the person wants to work
for you. Dealing with the high attrition rates is related to how
much of a personal connect the manager builds with his team
and how wanted employees feel at the organization.'

In a relationship-oriented culture, the boss has to make an
effort to connect with his team. There needs to be continuous
engagement either through one-on-one or group meetings. But it
goes beyond that. A factor that helps retain employees is making
them feel that they 'matter'.

People here like and look forward to celebrations, whether
it's festivals or small wins. If a job is done well or if monthly
targets are achieved, it could be celebrated with a lunch,

distribution of sweets or going out for drinks. These are ways to include the team and share the success; they help to create an attachment with the organization and positively impact employee engagement.

Susanne elaborates on this culture of celebration:

> One of the things that I love is the culture of celebration and recognition. An example is in the recruitment team. They have put a bell up on the wall, and whenever an offer to a candidate is made, someone goes and rings it. Everyone stands up and cheers, and whoever has made the offer tells them what's happened.
>
> There's a lot of celebration and very open recognition when people do well, and it's much, much more than in any other culture I have been part of before. A comparison for me would be the UK environment. There is recognition, but it's often a much more personal thing there. And here there's a lot more visual recognition – something that people can take away and be proud of and show their families. 'I've passed this and got a certificate' or 'I got a T-shirt or something that sets me apart from other people!'

Lending a helping hand

If there is genuine rapport and connect between people, they will go beyond what is expected in order to help. A young co-founder of a start-up says, 'There may not be infrastructural support in our space but there is people support. If one is able to alleviate that "stranger" feeling when meeting someone new, find something in common and connect with a person, he or she will go out of their way to help.'

And here it's relevant to mention that for the sake of the relationship and in order to accommodate requests, inconveniences are ignored and plans are put aside. Sometimes this is done as part of a job or process; at other times it's done despite the process.

Personal trumps process

Fiona Reynolds, an experienced international educator, shares this experience:

> Our flight back to Mumbai from the US was delayed in New York for hours, so naturally my husband and I were afraid we would miss our flight from Europe to Mumbai. We ran through the airport to try to make our connection. We got to the gate, but it was closed; however, the flight staff were still there. Breathlessly, we asked if we could still get on the flight. A lady from the host country said we couldn't as the gate was closed and, by policy, they couldn't open the door – even though we could see the plane, sitting quietly at the gate.
>
> Luckily for us, one of the check-in staff was from India. She took in our sad, tired and frustrated faces and said, 'I think we can get you on.' She had the gate reopened, and we got to board the flight (which was then delayed for a different reason). I appreciated that people trumped the procedure/process!

What is also worth noting in this example is that the Indian lady who got the gate reopened was not based in India but overseas. Some aspects of one's culture are ingrained.

Now, let's consider this rather mundane example: Mr Jain, a businessman, goes to his bank for some urgent paperwork that would normally take a couple of days. He doesn't know anyone at the bank in particular. He asks the manager for some documents that he needs urgently as he has to submit these to his chartered accountant. The bank manager, Mr Rathod, asks him to come after two days as the process needs a bit of time. Now, let's consider a situation where Mr Jain, being a long-term client, knows Mr Rathod and approaches him for this paperwork. The process still has to be followed, but now the tone and tenor change. Mr Rathod instructs or requests his team to look into and expedite the request; what's more, he offers Mr Jain the convenience of the documents being delivered to his house so that he doesn't have to make the trek to the bank again.

In other countries, if there is a process, it has to be followed. Irrespective of whom you know at the bank, exceptions are not usually made. Such a situation seems unlikely in New York; I cannot imagine this happening in Singapore.

So, things get worked around in India. I am not referring to a flagrant breaking of rules, but to the slight tweaking of rules and bypassing of the procedure. Things are often 'adjusted' in India in order to accommodate requests and favours for friends, relatives, colleagues and perhaps clients.

But there is a flip side to this: dealing with expectations. Sometimes, because of the relationship, there is an expectation that one will informally connect with his colleague to get the job done.

A friend remarks, 'If you have a prominent position in an organization, it is common for relatives, friends and even people who don't know you well to pick up the phone and seek a favour as they feel that you will be able to help. My cousin asked me if I could help my nephew Sunil get a job in my organization. I sent his contact details to my HR department, which in turn called Sunil for an interview. They found that while Sunil had strong IT skills, they were not a good match for the jobs in our organization. They arranged a meeting where they advised him to apply to another organization where his skills would be a better fit.'

What the example above highlights is that while favours are sought, and requests made (that aren't always reasonable), one doesn't always have to accommodate them or bend over backwards. One can help to the extent possible and with empathy, keeping in mind the organization's policies.

A point to note here is that while relationships matter, the friendly and familiar approach works only up to a point. As mentioned earlier, a balance between an authoritative and caring outlook is ideal. As James, who has moved out of India, remarks: 'People are going to like it if you are approachable. However, if you are too approachable or familiar, people may lose respect. If I had to do it again, I would have been more formal and used some of my authority outside my vertical.'

The friendly Indian: The good, bad and the ugly

Hands down, almost every expatriate I spoke to found Indians to be 'friendly'. They felt Indians were warm, considerate, wanting to help. But while this may be true from the lens of a foreigner, 'friendly' is not a word I would use to describe fellow Indians, at least not when one meets them initially. Often people don't acknowledge or greet each other with a 'Hello' or 'Good morning'. Those who do not know each other will seldom exchange words or a smile.

But as one goes beyond the basics, Indians open up and then it is a different story. Ashish makes this astute observation: 'I would say that Indians are a lot friendlier – but once you have scratched the surface. When you live overseas, the surface is a lot friendlier; when you scratch it, you don't always get the depth of friendship. It is more superficial but much more polite.'

In India, the reverse is true: as one goes beyond the surface, there is warmth, affection – often in abundance! It is no surprise then that for the expatriates I spoke with, one of the biggest positives of being in India is the people.

Building and sustaining networks

Given the importance of relationships, Indians devote considerable time and energy in forging networks. One can say that networking is part of the character of an average Indian!

David (name changed), an expat from Switzerland who has worked in different roles and assignments in India, shares his perspective on the importance of good working relationships in India:

> In a country, if you don't have the right network or relationship, you will not reach targets, whether it's in business or public service. You need a certain relationship management and the network which would let you access certain areas that you as a westerner may not be able to access. I got access to government bodies and to very high-level influential people in India, which from my own position I would not otherwise get. The degree of intensity of social activities is definitely higher here. It's also a requirement from the Indian side; I think the Indian mindset wants to have a good network.

In India, having a good network is necessary and making the right connections can be the key. The required time and efforts need to be expended in this regard.

Sometimes tapping into one's college network can facilitate getting that appointment, job or contract. However, this is not unique to India. The alumni of any institution, whether it is Harvard, Columbia or closer home the Indian Institutes of Management, have incredible networks which get tapped into. What is perhaps unique to India is the ties that bind these alumni. I have seen how my husband's batchmates have sustained these friendships over twenty-odd years. Despite being spread out all over the world, they make the time to meet one another. And they help one another in times of need.

This is also borne out in Chloe's observation: 'My dad went to IIT Madras and he graduated in the 1970s. His batchmates are like family. In my time in Mumbai, I could call them and they would be here in a minute to take me to the hospital. Indian classmates' networks are so different from those overseas!'

Relationships and networks are not just built but sustained too. In India, the relationship is invested in and nurtured, and doesn't end once the business ends. For instance, many months after we concluded our real estate deal, we received a box of the most delicious motichoor laddoos from our real estate agent. In fact, gifts of mangoes, silverware, dried fruit and chocolates are routinely sent by business associates on Diwali or other occasions. The surprising thing is that some of these associations may have been for just one transaction, but the gifts are sent year after year to keep the relationship going.

Regarding this culture of giving gifts, Virginia, says:

I can't go on a trip and not bring something back. Because the lady who makes tea at our office gets me some cashew nuts from her hometown, Ratnagiri. Someone will go to Gujarat and bring me a necklace.

It's gifts, gifts, gifts and it's quite hard to keep up. So the extent of it is different from what is seen in the UK or elsewhere.

Hospitality

Indians are on an extreme end of the spectrum when it comes to being hospitable. 'Atithidevo bhava', or the guest is the equivalent of God, is a belief held throughout the country. Even if one drops by, unannounced, to a person's house, one thing is certain: he will not leave without being offered at least a cup of tea.

Simon makes this observation: 'I've made and met Indian friends who would invite you to do things or to come home. In many Asian countries, that doesn't happen. People there are very nice and friendly, but you would never get asked to come around.'

This is the experience of Richard van der Merwe, a Senior Director of a large life sciences company. Based in India presently, he was here more than twenty years ago too. While many things have changed between then and now, some things are the same:

I was in Delhi for six weeks in 1994. The regional manager at the time invited me to his home for dinner. His daughter had just got married. I was at his home and it's something that I will never forget. It was a real experience!

Twenty-two years later I come back to India. The regional manager has been retired now for many years; he heard that I was back in India and he phoned me. He told me that the next time I am in Delhi, I must visit him. I did – it was an incredible experience! He literally rolled out the red carpet. I spent the entire evening there, was thoroughly entertained. I just had to eat and eat because they just give you so much and you have to try this and try that! They so appreciated the fact that I took the time and I didn't see it that way. That's Indian hospitality, warmth and kindness – it's very much there.

The flip side of people being friendly is that they may not be friendly for the right reasons. One expat said that people were so friendly that sometimes it made him wonder if there was a hidden reason. He says, 'With time, one learns to distinguish genuine kindness from interested flattering. Certain relationships are very much interest-driven. But that can be anywhere in the world.'

People can, and do, cross the line

The other aspect of being friendly is that curiosity goes hand in hand with it. People often take liberties and have no qualms about asking you all kinds of questions. Indians don't dwell on whether something may be appropriate or not for the other person. For instance, a few months ago at a social event, I met a person for the first time. Before I knew it, within minutes, he was asking me for my husband's contact details!

Then there are the questions about money matters. There is seldom much subtlety in this. Madhav, who returned to India after an overseas stint, narrates his experience:

People openly discuss salaries. Neighbours ask you, 'What's your pay, how much bonus did you get?' I just say that I don't talk about it, but if it's a close friend asking how much the house cost, you have to say something! They think it's conversation. A lot of private, unnecessary information gets asked. You could take offence

> or you could just brush it aside. It's not like the person asking the question cares. For them, it's like asking, 'How's the weather?'

While a foreigner will usually be spared the extent of this probing, the few questions that come his way would be enough to violate his personal space. However, the people I spoke to accepted this questioning as routine.

This is what Martin Bienz, the Consul General of Switzerland in Mumbai, says:

> Family is always a topic here, I think. If I meet somebody in my home country, he would not ask me: 'Are you married? How many children do you have?' But here this is a standard question. For instance, people are interested to know: 'Is he here alone in this country? Does he have his family with him?' I would say that's normal here. And I don't feel that it's too personal.

At times, the intrusion of personal space may be quite literal. Consider this comment from a Japanese interviewee: 'What struck me most was the lack of respect for personal space. Simple things like sharing the armrest on a flight or picking up the newspaper without permission from the neighbour's seat pouch are culturally different. While it seems very casual and completely acceptable in India, in Japan we are very cautious about the usage of shared space.'

Amy Sebes, an international school teacher and the spouse of a former US Consul General, shares her observations:

> I find people to be very friendly; I don't find them overfamiliar. The only situation that is unique about India is that people stand

very close to each other and I think that's because they are used to having so many people close to each other all the time. For foreigners, we are not used to that, so sometimes I'll be talking to someone and literally he's *this* close, and just for my own comfort I take a step back.

How have people dealt with over-familiarity? One has to get used to dealing with this. People can choose to respond to what they want to. For instance, Rory Newcomb, an international school teacher, would be direct when faced with awkward questions, telling people that she wasn't willing to share something with them.

And sometimes it can be unpleasant, especially for children who may not have experienced this behaviour before. Josh Bishop, High School Principal, American School of Bombay, spoke of how people take pictures of him and his kids when they go out, and while his son is social and he would be okay with this, his daughter, being more reserved, would be fearful. But he says that he and his wife have explained to them that it all comes from a pure and honest space.

Trust at work

Let's move on to another area: that of building trust at the workplace.

Erin Meyer, an American author and professor who specializes in the field of cross-cultural management, in her book, *The Culture Map: Breaking Through the Invisible Boundaries of Global Business*, talks of two forms of trust that are inherent across the world – cognitive trust and affective trust:

Cognitive trust is based on the confidence you feel in another person's accomplishments, skills and reliability. This is trust that comes from the head. It is often built through business interactions: we work together, you do your work well and you demonstrate through the work that you are reliable, pleasant, consistent, intelligent and transparent. Result: I trust you.

Affective trust, on the other hand, arises from feelings of emotional closeness, empathy or friendship. This type of trust comes from the heart. We laugh together, relax together and see each other at a personal level, so that I feel affection or empathy for you and sense that you feel the same for me. Result: I trust you.

In India, affective trust works. Why bother to build this, given that it takes time and energy and may simply be out of character for some people? The short answer is: because in the long run it is worth it. There is more buy-in and commitment and a better work environment.

Given below are Rajan's insights based on his experience of working in India after working for several years in the US. For him, the difference between the two work cultures is that between 'Tell me' and 'Trust me':

Unless you make employees understand how important the date is by when the project is to be delivered, dates don't mean much in India. They can keep moving! The prevalent thinking is: 'It's okay, there's no problem.' 'Getting half the job done by the date is fine.' They say, 'Ho jayega' (it will get done), and because of the relationship factor, the guy will say, 'Trust me.' But nobody wants to live a life of uncertainty at work. I can't assume that he will do the job. It's okay that it will not be done, but tell me!

For people to avoid situations like the one above, it's important to build relationships of trust. The boss, whether Indian or expat, has to create a safe environment, one in which employees can approach the boss and have the comfort of knowing that they will not get ticked off or shouted at.

Joe King says, 'In a conversation, people tell you what they think you would like to hear rather than what they believe. With trust, this gets better. After several follow-up chats, they get to the issues they have.'

How does one build or create a safe environment? When a colleague suggests trying out something new which is good, Eric appreciates it publicly and shares it with the team so as to encourage similar participation from others. Joe supports employees through risks and initiatives that they have taken – even if they haven't succeeded.

Brendon Breen, Health Teacher and Technology Coach at an international school, points out, 'It is important to not get angry or upset with the bearer of bad news. I communicate that I am happy that I have found out that I have this problem and now I can fix this.' Rory sums it up well: 'If you are going to build capacity in a person, you have to build a relationship first. After that you have to empower them and also manage your expectations.' In this context, David shares his approach:

Creating trust is about being clear in your communication, clear in your leadership and being open to mistakes. I remember my assistant had once made a mistake about which I was really not happy. She was very upset and saying, 'I'm doing everything wrong.' I told her, 'No, you are allowed to make mistakes. You don't have to defend something which is obvious. Just say, "It's a mistake, I take accountability for it. The next time I will not do it like this."' That approach helps to build trust.

But, on a related note, Indian millennials are different. They don't take mistakes or failures so personally. Shanti points out: 'The attitude has changed. The younger generation is very unapologetic about failure. They are not saying, "Oh, I've failed, I'm sorry." Because they just view it as another learning opportunity.'

Building trust is a slow process. It is as important for the Indian boss as it is for the non-Indian one. What are some techniques or ways that can help forge that connect? I posed this question to the people I interviewed, and here are some of the responses I got:

- I used to spend time on the floor with the teams every week. Sometimes you can sense that things aren't right but people won't open up. You need to invest that time to build trust. Once you do that, people will share issues and concerns.
- I would have town halls and breakfast meetings with twenty-five random people and chat with them. I would ask people to drop the 'Mr' and 'Sir' before my first name.
- Previously, if I was leading a business meeting, I'd get straight down to the agenda. Here, increasingly I've realized that there's a really important part about relationship building, so I start the meeting by asking some more general questions about people's families or what they did on the weekend.
- When entering into a new work environment for a business meeting or some other interaction, usually, as a foreigner, you have to give your back story. I would be as transparent as possible with anyone I met about who I am, where I am from, why I'm in India, and everything else, and that usually served as a fast track to getting to know people. The other thing I observed is that being transparent and sharing personal information with people created an atmosphere of sharing in the workplace. People

were less likely to hide and hold on to things when they saw someone in a position of management being open and sharing information as well.

- Social occasions, such as company picnics and post-meeting cocktail dinners, helped me connect and communicate more openly with people.
- Showing emotion is a good way of building trust – for instance, showing when you are happy and appreciating the work others have done.
- I'm always with people. I am not in my cabin with the door closed. So people can come to me whenever they want. It's a little bit painful because they keep coming and asking me things! But I prefer that; things get done.
- If you participate in celebrations, you are more accepted.
- I often use cricket as a topic of conversation to break the ice.
- I spend a lot of time having conversations over 'chai' to get people to open up.

It's relevant to mention here that small talk isn't always 'small'. Sometimes it helps build a lasting rapport. So how is small talk in India different from that in Western cultures? Rajan, who has worked in the US, the Middle East and India, distils it well:

There is small talk in the US but the nature of it is very different. In the US, if people ask, 'How are you doing?' you say, 'Good,' and you move on. Nobody's expecting an answer like, 'Things are rough!' As you move eastwards, in the Middle East, one of the first things the locals will ask you is, 'Everything good at home?' or 'How is your family?' What that shows me, in some sense, is that while they are being warm, the implicit question is, 'Is your mind rested?'

In the West, hardly anybody is going to ask you this. It's almost like, 'I don't want to know what's going on in your house.' To me, as I adapted, knowing what is going on in someone's family is good for me so that I know he's not disturbed or distracted. I have seen in Indian companies, if somebody has a problem, the manager will go out of his way and say, 'Don't worry, we'll help you.' So you are automatically getting the person to be more focused.

Conclusion

To conclude, whether it's in the personal or business space, forging a relationship with people goes some distance in India. The boss or the manager, Indian or not, has to make a genuine effort to connect and not do this to 'tick a box'. Building rapport does not necessarily involve efforts that are big, bold or time-consuming. Small but well-meaning gestures like a short chat on the phone or over a cup of tea can also work.

However, it's important to be cognizant of the fact that while relationships matter, so does hierarchy. A balance has to be struck between these two.

Mary Kay Hoffman, an American who lived in Asia for twenty years, ten of which were in India working in international schools, shares an insightful view:

I think people will respond to the question 'How do you build rapport in India?' differently. There are people who move to India who do believe they are better, have higher status. Therefore, they treat people that way. Their answers to this question would be different from someone who sees himself as a guest, who is visiting, or someone who can learn from others.

My answer is that you build relationships with people as equals. And what you get from that depends on how you invest in that.

In the words of an Indian repatriate: 'Given that people are friendly and warm, it is important from the perspective of senior management to know how to harness that warmth and hospitality when one comes to work in this part of the world. With people being warm to you, your behaviour cannot be the same as it was in your home country. The sooner you adapt, the better it is for you to be successful here.'

The non-Indian needs to be cognizant that results, deliverables, tasks and facts all matter, but so do people. It is important to recognize that both the rational and the relationship-centred approaches work in organizations and cultures. But while in India or working with Indians, knowing what works more and adapting to it can be a game changer.

3

Work and Life

In India, to a large extent, work is life.

This is true of the average, middle-class person from Generation X working in professional organizations, and it is truer of the preceding generations. Their work means a lot to them; they derive their identity solely, or largely, from it. They are conscious of their professional achievements, acutely aware of their roles and wear their titles proudly on their sleeves.

In an article titled 'Where rank alone matters' published in the *Times of India* in 2005, journalist Sunanda K. Datta-Ray, writes, 'India is not a country for the anonymous. You must be somebody to survive with dignity. Rank is the only acceptable substitute for money.'

This chapter looks at the role of work in the life of an average middle-class Indian employee. It also fleshes out his way of working and discusses the attitudes towards working women here.

Learn and live

'There is this voracious appetite for learning. Indians revere education,' says Craig, who has seen this up close from his position as head of an international school.

Indians *do* place a huge premium on education. A good education is viewed as a gateway to a successful career and life. This results in a child being saddled with high expectations and pressures – from his acceptance to a good school in kindergarten until he graduates from college. And so, one learns early on to strive hard to inch forward and make room for oneself in a highly competitive environment.

After one's graduation or postgraduation, landing a job is the much hankered-for 'reward'. The first job is often seen as a validation of the young adult's efforts and merit. Parents and well-wishers laud the young one for his success while, at the same time, telling him that this is just the beginning – he has to work hard. In India, a bright career paves the way for brighter marital prospects. Thus, society, or large sections of it, constantly encourages, supports and reinforces the message that working hard is good and necessary for a successful life.

One of the factors that contribute to this mindset is that, in India, the demand for every resource far outstrips the supply. For instance, housing in the bigger cities is ridiculously expensive, so people have to work hard to be able to afford a house. Another important point to bear in mind is that there are no government-sponsored medical or social security schemes, like those in the West, which assure one of a comfortable life post retirement. And so, people are consumed with the struggle to do well in one's career.

So, for a majority of working-class Indians, living is primarily about working. As Parag Jain, a compliance consultant, says succinctly: 'Work takes up a large part of the time-space and mind-space of an Indian.'

Hard work and the Indian

'To get a foothold in the bus you have to work hard from an early age, so it's ingrained in us,' says Rajesh. 'That applies to our academic and work life, where we have to compete far more than our counterparts overseas. I think we have a lot more quality talent willing to work harder to get the results.'

Indians are ambitious and aspirational – and are willing to put in the effort needed to succeed. This is often translated into long hours at work. Shanti offers this viewpoint: 'If you put an Indian in a competitive scenario, he will excel. Because there are two faces of India: one is the aspiring, developed, educated set of people who have access to more opportunities. And they are constantly in touch with the part of society that isn't as privileged (like drivers and maids). Because of this constant interaction, we don't take a lot of things for granted. We are fighters, we work hard.'

Anand Sanghi, President, Asia market, at Vertiv, who has over twenty years of experience in the Asia-Pacific region, helps put this in perspective:

Indians are definitely motivated to succeed. There's a strong drive and ambition. When you see some of the people in our generation who have been successful, we had some common traits: simple upbringing, good family values, focus on education. We understood that results come with dedication and investing time at work.

Indians are definitely hard-working. Having said that, I don't think the Chinese or the Koreans or the Japanese are any less so. But, for them, money may not be so important. For Indians, promotions, success, power and money are all important. So I think Indians are a lot more driven to get the trappings of growth and success.

In this context, Sangeeta, whose colleagues from Latin America work on weekends too, feels that working hard is a 'developing market' thing, not just an Indian thing.

I recently conducted a training assignment for an American who had several years of experience working in Europe, the Middle East and East Asia. He made an interesting observation with regard to the Indian work ethic: 'I wish I could bottle the Indian's commitment, motivation and dedication and spray it over my people back home!'

But, while Indians work hard, do they work smart? An expat says, 'I think people are very committed at heart and want to do well. However, this is expressed in different ways that don't translate well across cultures. Staying back in the office might be seen as commitment by one person and a lack of ability to do one's job by another.' Notwithstanding the long hours spent at work, the day may not be very productive due to the tendency to take frequent breaks from work or, in some cases, attend meetings that don't serve much purpose.

Rajan shares his views on the matter:

One cannot generalize about Indians being more committed. But I feel that a large percentage of people are very committed to their work. They feel it's important for them to do what they are told to do. Indians are very emotional and they don't treat their job as a job.

In the West, people structure their day – these are one's work hours, family hours, sleep hours. In the case of Indians, they will do whatever it takes to give the most to their work. They are okay with putting in fifteen hours of work a day. But the problem is that while they put in fifteen hours of work, they may not be putting in that many hours of productivity.

Peter makes a relevant point: 'At times, there is a sense that hard work matters more than results. For instance, a person in my team will tell me, "I worked all weekend, I couldn't finish the project or task, but I worked all weekend." I care less about how many hours he worked, I care about the results. And if he gets the results working fewer hours, that's even better!'

Related to the point about working on weekends, this is Hari's observation:

Indians are very hard-working and try to be team players. They will step into the breach, burn the midnight oil, and shoulder additional responsibilities without immediate expectations of recognition or reward. Working over a weekend, even Sunday, is par for the course. In the West, that simply wouldn't work. It would have to be positioned as a one-off, be time-bound, and the rewards formalized prior to the engagement.

Conversely, deny an Indian his recognition or reward, and you will never hear the end of it. They will bring it up persistently and at every opportunity till the matter is resolved. But it is not unusual to see Indians sacrifice a great deal of home life to work.

This trait of Indians putting in extra hours at work at the cost of their personal or family time leads to the next topic.

Merging of the professional and the personal

In India, the division between one's professional and personal lives is not a clear one. It's not like people will look at their watches at 6 p.m. on a workday and say, 'Okay, I have done my "work", now it's my "personal" time.' One does not end nor does the other begin so definitively. People may continue to be on work-related calls while commuting or go home and work on that urgent project report. Bosses may not think twice about phoning their subordinates late in the evening – or even at night.

Even on a weekend, this spillover continues. Rajesh, who heads a large organization, says, 'On weekends too, I work. That's true for a lot of people at my organization. It's partly because that's the nature of working in India and partly because culturally nobody respects your time. There is no such thing that people will not call you on the weekend. I get calls from anyone at work who has a problem or someone from the industry in case of a development. Overseas, nobody would call me over the weekend, unless he was a very close friend.'

As Ashish remarks: 'People try and push their way through, so it's a bit of an in-your-face culture at work. By that I mean it's an intrusive work culture.'

This is not to say that this spillover does not happen in other places and cultures. A close friend of mine, who is a successful head of research at a global financial services firm in the US, goes home by 6 p.m., puts the kids to bed and then catches up on work-related matters. As do countless people with stressful and demanding jobs. But the extent of this spillover is far greater in India. Here, one's job and one's personal life blend. Unapologetically. Constantly.

This tendency is evident in this anecdote narrated by an expat from Europe:

My Indian colleague Ashok (name changed) was on leave. However, he learnt later that his boss from abroad was planning to visit his office during the period of his leave. Ashok took a break (from his 'break') and came to the office for the duration of his boss's visit. It may have helped that he wasn't travelling and was at home.

Notwithstanding this, in my country, people would look at Ashok like, 'Have you lost your mind? If I'm on vacation, I don't care whether it's the king or queen; I'm not going to be at the office!'

Ashish, who has worked with people from different cultures in his stints abroad before repatriating, makes an interesting observation: 'The overseas work culture is cut and dried. I am here to do a job, I do it, I get up at the end of the day and then I go home and this part is shut off. That doesn't happen here. People carry their work with them all the time.'

Related to this point about people carrying their work, I would like to share something I have observed often. At dinner parties, Indians – and this is truer of men than women – tend to talk shop. They talk about business issues, trends, impact, business challenges, etc., notwithstanding that it's the end of a week and they are with their spouses. This view is shared by a senior Indian manager, who, as a woman, makes this perceptive observation:

For Indians, a dinner with colleagues is not just about eating and letting one's hair down. After two drinks, the guys start talking about some aspect of their work, their role or some challenge that they face. Whereas when I am with non-Indians over a three-hour dinner, they tend to talk about lighter topics. It could be about someone's kids, someone's dog or someone's cow. That's what dinner table conversation is! If somebody gets into work areas, people will push them back, saying, 'This is dinner time, don't talk about work.' In India it will never be like that. I can't imagine a three-hour dinner with colleagues where work is not discussed.

And speaking of dinner parties, often there is a more literal compartmentalization. Lorna, a South African expat, says, 'When we have cocktail parties, or company functions with spouses, the spouses sit in one corner and the men sit together. It's tough for us (spouses of expats). I don't know where to go because there is a group of Indian ladies who perhaps know each other and you've got to push your way in there. And they are nice but they don't think they need to mix with or meet the men. I would like to meet everyone!'

The fun factor

Mukesh makes this observation after repatriating to India, 'At work, there's more humour. On a typical working day, you will laugh more often.'

There may or may not be more humour but there is definitely more social interaction at work. People eat lunch together, often sharing their 'dabba' or 'tiffin'. Updates on movies and in-laws are shared, jokes are exchanged and forwarded. There is constant interplay between work and the personal. It is common to have friends at work. In fact, for many people the only friends they have are those from the workplace. Susanne shares an anecdote:

There was an interesting question I came across in the Employee Engagement Survey: 'Do you have friends at work?' It made me smile. And I remember thinking, 'Gosh, I've never been asked that before, especially in the context of a work-related engagement survey.'

But it's something that's really important here and I see it all around me. When I talked to a couple of people about it, they felt that if they didn't have close friends at work, they wouldn't enjoy work at all. They made it very clear that they meant friends and not just good colleagues. It's really interesting that a sign of engagement here is that people have close friends at work. It shows just how important relationships are in all aspects of life here.

I have made close friends at work over the years. In the West, at the end of the day or over lunch, we might all come together for a chat as friends, but during the day we are all working. It's segmented, I guess. But here friendship is an incredibly important part of work itself.

And it's not just colleagues who become friends. Clients become friends, friends become clients.

The social aspect of working in India is elaborated upon here by two interviewees:

One of the positive aspects when you come here from abroad and work in an office in India is that the people are friendlier. In general, the atmosphere at an Indian workplace is warm. People are more engaged with each other. It's not quite like a college campus but the camaraderie is similar.

But socializing at work and after work is relative. It is difficult to generalize because it really comes down to the individuals. Also, it comes down to how much workload there is. The youngsters who are fresh out of university hang out at the office till late and they socialize a lot. But anyone with a family, commitments and responsibilities wants to go home. Once in a while, it's like, 'Let's go for a drink or dinner,' but it's not too much.

Does the socializing impact delivery of tasks as per timelines? Scott says, 'The people here will have their forty-five-minute or an hour-long lunch break (even though there's a deadline tomorrow). They do work last minute, but they deliver, so that's not a worry for me. I have some guys who work until 10 or 11 p.m. That's their choice!'

But this can impact productivity, points out Rajan: 'The fun factor is good at work, but it can be a double-edged sword. It's good to be personally connected, but up to a certain point where it's still productive. We had situations where people were out for birthday parties even when there was a strict deliverable at work. It's not that it's wrong, but where do you draw the line? And how do you find the balance? That is very important.'

Work-life balance

The overlap between the professional and personal has a downside: it impacts work-life balance. The data below shows how India compares with other countries on the parameter of work-life balance:

Work-life balance across sixty-five countries, the Expat Insider 2017 survey report, published by InterNations

RANK	WORK-LIFE BALANCE
1	Denmark
8	The Netherlands

Rank	Work-Life Balance
17	Malaysia
20	Germany
30	Canada
39	The United Kingdom
40	Australia
47	China
48	The United States of America
52	The United Arab Emirates
58	India
61	Hong Kong
65	Japan

As can be seen from the table above, Denmark fares the best amongst the sixty-five countries on the aspect of work-life balance. India is amongst the lower ranking countries at 58; work-life balance in India is far from ideal. People work to live but also live to work. Work does not just entail spending long hours at the office. Many people in the metros stay a considerable distance from their offices, and it takes them anywhere from an hour to three to and from the office, so a large part of their day is spent commuting.

Virginia says, 'I have tremendous respect for people who get on a train or a bus every single day and travel two or three hours. I think, considering the heat, pollution and noise, people are tremendously hard-working, not out of choice perhaps, but out of necessity.' And in this context are Hari's comments: 'The Mumbaiwallah walks long distances to work even if it means getting drenched and hugely delayed. It's an astonishing demonstration of commitment to work but typical of the culture.'

For many people, the job is their primary or only focus. This is probably truer for men than women. In the case of the latter, they are often saddled with the additional responsibilities of running home and hearth. All these factors take a toll on people's emotional and physical well-being. People work here to the detriment of their health. Needless to say, given the long work hours, travel times and constraints, work-life balance is more often than not skewed in favour of more work and less play.

Much of this, though, doesn't apply to the millennials. Shanti, who interacts a lot with this generation of Indians by virtue of her profession as an angel investor, makes a relevant point: 'How things have changed over the last twenty-five years! Our parents stayed in the same job for decades. Our generation moved away from that and started doing different things every five years. This generation is doing things for one or two years and they feel, "Wow, I've already worked so hard!"'

Staying connected 24x7

In an increasingly interconnected world, people are constantly checking their phones for messages, emails and social media updates. In India, this may be more of a preoccupation than elsewhere. Whether this is because of the convergence of the professional and personal or other factors, the Indian and his phone don't seem to stay separated for too long.

As mentioned earlier, work calls are not off-limits over the weekend. Another way in which communication is different here, as pointed out by an Indian who has worked overseas, is the 'humongous' use of texts and WhatsApp at work.

On a related note, here's an amusing anecdote as narrated by an expatriate:

> When I came here, I was impressed by how business people can spend four days at a wedding – in the middle of a week. But they

still manage their operational activities. That's why maybe Indians are more on their phones in any situation. For example, when we were in Delhi, my wife was a member of the international women's club. There was once a lady speaker on stage giving a speech and, in the middle of her talk, her mobile began ringing. You will not believe it, this lady, who had the phone with her, answered the call and talked to the caller while on stage!

In an Expedia survey conducted in 2015 to study mobile-device-related behaviour and preferences among travellers across nineteen countries, it was found:

India leads globally, with 80 per cent of the participants stating that they check in on work at least once daily while on holiday. India is followed by Thailand (74 per cent) and Mexico (65 per cent) . Travellers from Germany, Norway and Sweden tend to be less reliant on their devices compared to other countries.

Responding to emails

Given the above, it should come as no surprise that it is common for people to write and respond to emails over the weekend. This is not a habit or trait found only in Indians. People who work in other countries do check their emails when not in office, but it's usually limited to urgent matters and not done with the same intensity or sense of priority.

As Sangeeta says, 'In India, the approach is, "I will have lunch or dinner with my family when I will not look at my emails – that's work-life balance!" Of course, this also depends on the nature of the role one has in an organization.'

Ashish remarks, 'When I worked overseas, I hardly ever received emails on the weekend. But here I constantly receive emails on the weekend, even from my team. Sometimes they are under pressure and catching up on their mails, but there are times when they are not under pressure and are responding to mails out of habit. So I get a good thirty to forty emails over the weekend, and if I choose to respond, I will get a reply almost immediately.'

To my question, 'Do Indians respond quickly to mails that you send?' Justin, a manager from New Zealand, replied, 'Yes, very quickly. They must be on email all day and night! I don't answer mails on weekends, but I get them.'

This is Peter's viewpoint: 'I discourage people working on weekends. One thing that really annoys me is when people send emails on weekends, especially when they can wait till Monday. If someone wants to work on the weekend, that's their choice; I am not going to stop them. But what I'd prefer them to do is save their mails as drafts and then send them on Monday morning. When they send emails on weekends, they make other people feel that they should be working on weekends.'

Sateen points out that this tendency could at times be a bit in the nature of showmanship, to just make the point – "I am working" – as compared to actually giving some useful information. 'For instance, somebody responds with, "I'll get back to you," which on a Sunday is pointless because nobody is really going to get back to you on a Sunday!'

Rational and traditional

Not only are Indians able to juggle and switch between the professional and the personal but they are also adept at balancing the rational and the traditional. This happens in a seamless way, such that it may not even be noticed as something special.

Indians bring religion into work. Often people will have an idol or a picture of their deity on their desks, observe fasts and go to their place of worship on the way to work. 'As to the combination of spirituality with business,' Martin Bienz observes, 'a businessman sitting in front of you in a suit is Western in the way he dresses and behaves. And then he goes to attend a ceremony for a factory opening or participates in a ground breaking or bhoomi pujan ceremony. Both go parallel; one does not exclude the other, which I find fantastic!'

There is the business tycoon who has hired the best global consultant to overhaul the systems and processes, yet who will hire a Vaastu expert to help him plan an optimum office layout. One sees the CEO who is used to taking independent decisions in a jiffy but will defer to his mother as to which day to move into his new house.

An expat, over his long stint of working and living in India, observes:

> I think the emotional aspect is definitely different in India compared to the more rationally behaving societies. In my world, religion and spirituality are private and do not belong to the corporate world. Indians have a higher ability to combine emotional elements with rationalism. The emotional and the rational fit together very well here.

Attitude towards working women

A book on the cultural nuances of working with Indians would be incomplete without some words on how Indian women working in organizations are perceived.

The attitude towards the working woman ranges from the archaic to progressive and everything in between, depending on the city or town she is in, the culture of the organization and the people around. Of course, there are plenty of women who are successful and strong and push the limits every day and have wonderful careers. But not all women are empowered or equal.

Let's look at a few relevant themes that are specific to working women. One aspect is that of identity. I recall, when I was working in a consultancy firm in Singapore and I would meet with clients who were Indian, within a few minutes they would ask me what my husband did. The reverse never happened, with people asking my husband what I did. This has been not just my experience but that of many others.

A woman's success is often qualified. As Kanchana says:

If a woman is successful, people attribute her success to factors other than herself or her talent. There is always a rejoinder like, 'She had a great male mentor,' or 'Her family or husband is very supportive.' It's rarely just, 'She's a fabulous HR director or savvy sales person.'

While there isn't much of a bias about hiring women, the problem is in assigning roles to them. Women are preferred in roles like HR or administration – more transactional and less strategic roles. If a woman is considered for a role that is for some reason perceived to be one that only a man can do, incredulous statements like 'You think a woman can do this?' will be asked.

Often women must prove that they are worth listening to; they have to work twice as hard to be heard. While the reverse is not true, mansplaining is the norm.

While Indian women undoubtedly have the larger role to play domestically, it doesn't mean that they assume subservient roles at work or that they are not confident and assertive. On the contrary, many of the expats I spoke with found them very competent and confident.

'I think most women here have a great deal more pressure than those in Western societies. Lots of expectations are put on them in terms of managing the house, children, their husbands and everything else, and yet they accomplish so much,' says Carrie Udeshi, an intercultural consultant based in India for more than a decade.

James observes, 'Because of that superior place that men have, women doing more transactional roles would tend to be subservient or shy. But the ones in leadership roles, they weren't any different from the ones in the US.'

The above notwithstanding, there is an unfortunate mindset discussed below:

Susanne shares that she has heard statements like, 'There's no point saying that she's high potential because she is getting married next year.' She's had to step in and remind people that someone's home life and whether they are getting married or not is not relevant when they are talking about her potential to grow and develop.

Unfortunately, this mindset is prevalent. It is a reflection and extension of how the Indian woman is viewed. And it persists despite efforts to have more diversity. An expat comments, 'We do diversity workshops, we have cultural workshops. During discussions, all the men I work with will say, "Yes, yes yes," but at the end of the day when I say to them, "Why did you not employ a woman, why did you go and employ a male once again?" I get such a long story about "Maybe she will get pregnant" or "Maybe she's got her home to look after" and a whole host of reasons as to why they would prefer to have men rather than women.'

Also, security concerns impact the hiring of women. Eric says, 'We have three shifts. As the night shift is not possible for women, we have fewer of them. But we are exploring solutions to hire more women.'

Even today, whether you are in Delhi or Mumbai, a village or a tier-2 city, a temple or a nightclub, the rules for women aren't the same as those for men. If a woman has a couple of drinks with her colleagues, it could be completely cool in the media or advertising worlds, but in the more traditional sectors it may still be frowned upon or criticized.

Other aspects are commented upon too. A senior Indian executive says, 'How women dress is a huge discussion point. I've been privy to comments like, "She wears dresses to work," or, "She is not professionally dressed for a board meeting." I can't fathom how men can decide what's appropriate for women. Curiosity around a woman's marital status baffles me. If she is single or divorced, she is subjected to greater scrutiny than her single or divorced male colleague. The one thing that bothers me in India is this lack of respect for privacy and intrusive questions about personal lives.'

Anand puts this in perspective: 'It's important to understand that the code of conduct and the rules of behaviour for men and women, while they are changing now, are not exactly the same. Though women are in senior positions and are growing more in the hierarchy, the whole thing about drinking, smoking and socializing is very different. Also, there is the aspect of a handshake versus a hug – there are no separate rules around this and that's what probably throws foreigners off. Like, in some countries, it's totally taboo, but in India it's neither here nor there. You could have somebody who is very polished, who has had a drink or two with you, is willing to joke and chat, but at the same time, in another context, wants to just say, 'Namaste,' or shake hands and make sure that there's nothing more than that. India is many countries and many cultures in one; you can't apply one rule to everyone!'

Conclusion

Indians are complex, with multiple drivers of thinking and behaviour operating at different levels. In the words of an interviewee, 'In India, we struggle with a work culture that is influenced by traditional Indian society. In fact, most of the differences in work culture that set us apart from the rest of the world are fallouts of how we exist and behave in the Indian ecosystem.'

I hope that by putting these behaviours and attitudes in context, the reader gets a better understanding and appreciation of the average Indian's approach to work and why he behaves the way he does.

People would do well to be cognizant of some of these nuances and find their way of working around them in order to be effective here. Given the mindset and approach to work, the expat or repatriate boss would do well to establish and explain his style of working and expectations. This could include his preferences regarding receiving emails over the weekend!

4

Shades of Grey

The Articulate Indian

At the risk of stereotyping a nation of a billion-plus people who speak in regional languages and have diverse accents, fluency in English may not be the norm but it's not the exception either.

There is English...

First things first – the language introduced to India by the British has been embraced and has over the years become not only the lingua franca in the business world but also the language of choice among sections of the urban populace.

Given that India has several dialects and that most Indians are proficient in at least two Indian languages, the average Indian's fluency and grasp of the English language is no mean achievement. Well-educated Indians are extremely articulate, able to express themselves clearly and confidently in English. Those from smaller towns may not have the same degree of proficiency; some can communicate to the extent of getting their message across.

In the larger cities, people at work largely speak in English despite their diverse mother tongues. So does that mean communication is fairly simple and straightforward? On the face of it, yes. Day-to-day communication for business purposes does not pose challenges due to the language issue. But there are other aspects and nuances that do. This chapter attempts to address these areas lest they needlessly confound, worry or add a shade or two of grey to one's tresses!

...and then there is Indian English

The first thing that people may notice is that while English used in India is similar to that used internationally, there are some local hues. An interviewee said, 'One of the biggest challenges here is the communication. Because it's in English, many people feel that it's easy to understand, which is not (entirely) true.'

Some years ago, I was invited to a dinner party hosted by my friends Amitabh and Deepali (all names have been changed) in Singapore. Amitabh, who is a director of a US-based hedge fund, had invited some friends from his condominium. Amongst them were some Indian friends, who were also in the finance sector, and a few Caucasians. I was chatting with Alex, an Australian who had recently moved to Singapore from Belgium, and Radhika, an Indian who was working in Amitabh's office. Radhika and I were talking along the usual lines: when did I move to Singapore, was I working, was she there with her family, which Indian city were we both from. When we realized that we were both from Mumbai, the inevitable question came up: which college did she *pass out* from?

Alex immediately jumped into the conversation with: 'What do you mean you *passed out* of college?' Both Radhika and I were taken aback. What kind of a question was that? It was only much later that I realized where Alex was coming from, and that we had used an incorrect phrase that we had, not for a moment, felt was out of place. And we weren't the exception either; there are several thousands of Indians who, even today, use it.

This is just one example of English spoken by Indians. Consider this comment:

> I do not think Indians are good at English. The pronunciation is very different from British and American English. They think that they are good at English but the grammar is not so good.

The irony is that this observation was made by a person from a country not known for its English skills. However, the point is taken!

Another tricky area is that of regional accents. Indians grapple with how their fellow Indians pronounce certain words in their regional accents. Some communities have been and continue to be the object of much ridicule. Then there is the aspect of the speed at which many Indians speak English. Susanne says, 'With regard to Indians talking fast, I am getting used to it! To begin with, I found it difficult. But in the same way, people find my accent quite difficult. It's about speed, intonation and sometimes volume.'

Communicating: The Indian way

Before discussing how Indians communicate, it may be a good idea to look at the bigger picture: how similar are Indians to other Asians in their approach? One thing is certain: not all Asians can be painted with the same brush when it comes to communication. Of the Asian countries I am familiar with, the Japanese are at one end of the spectrum, with their highly nuanced, subtle and indirect style of communication. Indonesians, Filipinos and Thais are polite and respectful. Singaporeans are more direct and a bit clinical.

This is an Asian's take on communication styles in countries that he has lived in:

In the countries where I've worked earlier – Belgium and Germany – communication is content-driven, rational and logical; it's all black and white. Coming to this part of the world, Singapore is similar. With Indonesians, you have to find out what they want to say. Filipinos are also somewhat communicative but less than Indians.

Research in the cross-cultural domain indicates that Indians, are 'high' on context when it comes to communication. High-context cultures are those where communication is more implicit, subtle and layered. In India, while people are generally polite and reticent, they can also be expressive and fairly direct, more so than in many of the Asian countries mentioned above. As Kevin remarks, 'I think Indians are both context- and content-oriented. You need a mix of both approaches; you cannot be only content-oriented or rational here.'

Consider Virginia's perceptions on how Indians communicate:

Communication in India is incredibly direct and there's almost no filter. So, if you're looking tired, you'll be told you're looking tired and 'Are you ill?' If you've put on a little bit of weight, people will say, 'What happened, yeah?' or they will say, 'You've become fat.' So it's very to-your-face. It's very different from the rest of South-East Asia, which is much more aware of hierarchies in society and respect for elders. There is that in India obviously, but I would say communication is very direct.

However, while people may communicate their thoughts and opinions, there is one caveat: the hierarchy factor which impacts and dilutes directness socially and professionally, as elaborated upon in the 'Yes Boss' chapter. But as Indians feel comfortable with their colleagues and bosses, they share their views. In fact, they may even take it to the next level!

Not always on point

So, while there is a penchant for talking, there is also is a tendency for people to not address the question asked. Or to briefly address the question and then digress. I witnessed this behaviour at a popular literature festival in Mumbai.

A well-known journalist and commentator was moderating a discussion on the role of the media in the world. He was in conversation with a senior American journalist. They discussed a wide range of topics – the 2016 elections in the US, the fallout, and in conclusion the journalist even commiserated with Hillary Clinton. During the Q&A session, a lady got up to make a point, one that resonated with many in the audience. She said, 'We had come to hear about media in the world but we only heard about media and political events in the US!' The suave Indian commentator immediately extended an apology, but added, 'In India, we are trained to not stick to the topic. As a moderator, it's almost a virtue!'

A common chord

Language is always a great connector and that is equally true in India. If two people from Kolkata working in a factory in Raipur meet and discover that they are from the same city or region, they may start talking in Bengali. I notice that when I use my half-baked knowledge of Gujarati while talking to a salesperson who knows the language, all of a sudden the equation changes. The other person becomes more receptive and there's more warmth. For this reason, sometimes it's a good idea to learn a few words in the dominant language of one's team.

One fallout of the huge diversity within India is that people have affiliations to their region, province, town, and so on, and this may result in a clannish tendency or a desire to hang out with and help one's 'own people'.

Moving on to a different aspect, consider the following scenario:

Two friends, Ashok and Madhavi, are chatting at a coffee shop in Mumbai. Ashok, a marketing executive, and Madhavi, a finance professional, are catching up as they are meeting after many months. Ashok, on hearing his name being called out, gets up to collect his order. As he waits at the counter, there is a tap on his shoulder and a loud 'Hey, man!' Turning slowly, he sees it is Ravi, his close friend from college. They chat for a few minutes and, since Ravi is alone, Ashok invites him to join him and Madhavi. The conversation then goes like this:

Ashok: Madhavi, meet my friend Ravi; we studied together. He is a corporate trainer. Ravi, meet Madhavi, my former colleague.

Ravi: Nice to meet you Madhavi. Ashok and I go back a long way. My God, it's been how many years since college – 12, 15…?

Ashok (interjecting): It feels like a lifetime, man. Those were the days; remember we used to go to Prithvi to watch plays and that Raj restaurant…

Madhavi: I know Raj. I live nearby but do you know it's closed down now? So Ravi, what areas do you train in?

Ravi: I train in areas pertaining to leadership development. You know, transformational leadership, coaching...

Madhavi (cutting him short): I should introduce you to my HR head – he is always looking for good trainers! In fact, we have...

Ashok (interjecting): Your HR guy will love Ravi. He is the best! Didn't you get your certification in coaching from an overseas institute?

Madhavi: Can you send me your contact details? I'll connect with you...

Conversations like the one above, whether social or at work, follow a similar pattern: where people talk more and listen less. This then brings us to the next nuance.

Are you listening?

Broadly speaking, Indians don't seem to share the same enthusiasm for listening as they do for talking. In debates and discussions, Indians talk without listening to what the other person is saying, very often cutting him off while he is in the middle of a sentence. However, where the rule of hierarchy is in play, people listen well. For example, when a boss or a senior person talks or instructs, or when a senior family member talks to youngsters.

Here are some observations about how Indians do – and often don't – listen!

This is what an Indian professional working in a multinational corporation says:

We are very poor listeners. In senior-level meetings, everyone wants to get heard, so the loudest voice gets heard first. That's a classical Indian phenomenon, about which an outsider who is visiting will say one of two things: 'Wow, such good quality of conversations and feedback, everybody wants to contribute,' or, 'How do you guys manage? Nobody is listening to the other person!'

Jos Hulsbosch, who was Chief Operations Officer at Union KBC Asset Management while in India, felt that in his interactions with people, he had to repeat instructions because people did not concentrate enough on what was being said.

An expat who has been in India for over ten years observes:

Indians like to talk, and what I've learned is to not get annoyed. Since there are so many people, you have to talk to get heard – no one's going to wait around for you. Once you understand that, you realize that nobody is cutting into your conversation. They just need to be heard. While I wouldn't say that Indians are great listeners, I have some friends who are!

Information in bits and pieces

Communication is often wanting when it comes to formalities and procedures in India. Take the situation of opening or closing a bank account. Often the complete information isn't given up front.

I have, as countless others must have, experienced that the banking staff, especially in government banks, ask you to furnish a couple of things like documents A and B and a couple of photographs. When one lands up with that, they say, 'Oh, we also need documents C and D.' Why wasn't this mentioned earlier? Probably an oversight or, more likely, the second time around you are dealing with another official who has a better sense of the requirements.

Unfortunately, this is the case in many situations – whether it's renewing a driver's licence or applying for a club membership.

Given the above-mentioned tendencies of not always being on point, selective listening and not giving the complete information, it's important to be attuned and ask questions proactively so as to fill in the missing gaps. One shouldn't assume that what is said is complete and final.

Emotions at work

In an article titled 'In India, emotions speak louder than words', published in *Mint* in February 2010, Aakar Patel talks about how Indians communicate simultaneously by word and gestures. For instance, an Indian may ask a waiter to refill his glass with water while holding it up. He reasons that this is the result of a society recently having become literate. 'Words hold less meaning in such a culture, and fewer ideas can be communicated through them alone. Because of this, our expression of emotion is more pronounced. The Indian bowler who has missed, the quiz contestant who gets it wrong, contorts his face or winces, exhibiting his distress more openly than would someone from European or even other Eastern societies. This reaction is involuntary and not easy to suppress, because it is cultural ... the emotion must be displayed quickly in the conversation so that the other person understands our view.'

It should come as no surprise then that this no-holds-barred expression of emotions occurs at the workplace too.

The head wag

Shaken, not stirred. An apple martini? No, something far more banal – the head wag, an essential part of the Indian's communication arsenal. It could be an indication of a 'yes' or 'no'. But it's seldom so simple. It could mean anything from 'I'm listening', 'I don't understand', 'You don't make sense', to 'I agree' and 'Yes, I like this idea, it's great!'

A person used to a direct verbal style of communication is unaware of how to read and interpret this complex aspect of body language. Here's Virginia's unique take on it:

> The head wag? I love it! In fact, I take it back to England with me. I find it easy to do, though it's taken me time to understand it. I think it's a really relaxed way of communicating – you don't always have to say 'yes'. To me, it means everything and nothing all at the same time. It means you're taking it in, you're absorbing what's being said, or you're not, or the other person is speaking rubbish!

It's relevant to mention here that Indians seldom express that they don't understand something. Raising one's hand and admitting ignorance or lack of comprehension, whether it's in a classroom or a board meeting, is not a common occurrence. Culturally, this has not been encouraged. Peter points out:

> Certainly the people we have here are quite bright and can communicate well. However, if someone doesn't understand me, they are very unlikely to tell me and I think that's a shame. If I was talking about something with a group of twenty people, and one of them raised their hand and said, 'Actually, I didn't understand, can you explain again?' I'd be really impressed with that person!

Hari shares this enlightening take on the 'nod': 'Most foreigners assume that it denotes understanding. Not quite. It may convey attentiveness and definitely respect. Bottom line, don't let it fool you. Converting instructions into action could be a challenge unless you probe into what has been understood and follow up. Once established, communication is less demanding, and productivity improves.'

Emails

Indians have a tendency to write lengthy, at times rambling, emails, which may be unclear and confusing. Kanchana elaborates on this: 'Indians tend to write emails often cloaked with superfluous words and complex sentences, so, at the end of a reading, I am not clear as to what is being said! More often than not, the email confuses and it does the exact opposite of what it is supposed to do, that is, convey with clarity. Junior staff write emails that reek of subordination, are copied to irrelevant people and do not follow simple rules of email etiquette. I have been told that I am too direct in emails to a peer or a senior. I didn't change my style; I truly believe an email should be precise and direct.'

Chris Rogers, Senior Executive at a large multinational financial services company, says, 'When people are conveying a message or idea, they tend to use a hundred words when ten will do. Similarly, when they write, I try to get people to be more concise and understand that when communicating with busy people, it's vital they get their message across quickly if they are to gain interest.'

But as Hari points out, 'Being to the point may actually be seen as a sign of rudeness and arrogance!'

Then there is the issue of timeliness in replying to emails. An Indian based overseas says, 'Of all the people I have dealt with, the Indians' response time to emails is terrible. You have to follow up with an SMS or a call.'

Communication in meetings

In general, most meetings have an element of small talk. I have been in meetings where small talk goes on for a long time, but the upside is that it can have a good impact on the business end of things. Indulging in small talk can be unsettling or annoying to a person from a more direct culture, but as one comes to terms with this behaviour, one will be able to appreciate that the ability to make small talk in business is a skill worth having in one's repertoire.

Active participation

As mentioned earlier, Indians are very happy to share their opinions, ideas and thoughts. This is apparent in meetings, particularly internal office meetings where usually there is active participation, high energy and loud engagement.

Susanne says, 'In meetings, there is a lot of really animated conversation. People talk at the same time, talk over each other, and from a cultural point of view I sometimes find that quite difficult. But, for my Indian colleagues, that doesn't seem to be an issue at all. Everyone seems to be able to listen to multiple conversations at the same time, which is a great skill to have! Meetings here are a lot louder than the ones I am used to!'

However, this isn't the case always. People may not talk much if they have inhibitions relating to communication, like not being conversant in English. And the hierarchy is a factor. Active engagement and participation happens in organizations where people feel comfortable to express themselves, where the culture permits them to.

Sticking to an agenda

In his understated, polite Japanese way, an interviewee says, 'Meetings may not be strictly agenda-bound and may deviate to other related topics at times. In Japan, meetings are kept as brief as possible with maximum pre-meeting preparation. In India, sometimes we have longish meetings.'

Whether it is an external or internal meeting, it could be a challenge to stick to a strict agenda in India. Meetings are often free-flowing, where one point can lead to another, which can then lead to a completely different subject. The conversation may digress and not follow a logical, linear line of thinking as highlighted in this anecdote shared by Kevin:

> I work for a German company; I have a military background, so I am used to a linear way of discussion. One goes from A to B to C and there is a certain structure in the way you plan the discussion. Here, it doesn't necessarily work that way.
>
> Let's say you have certain points to discuss for a contract. Instead of going in order, there is a tendency to interconnect everything. In the process, it gets more complicated!
>
> You can create a certain framework and say, 'Hey guys, can we discuss along these lines?' That works, but honestly speaking, after several years here, I got some feedback from my boss. He said, 'How come when you're explaining, you're not direct and to the point?' I think he was surprised because I'm normally a very direct person.
>
> When I told one of my close friends in the industry about this, he remarked 'Kevin, you're becoming an Indian now!'

Another nuance of communication in meetings is that there can be an analysis paralysis. This is narrated by a senior executive: 'What I do have a problem with sometimes is that they will make projects a lot more complicated than they actually are. I think people are innovative, but they are inclined to discuss simple things and over-analyse them. If I ask them, "Why don't we conduct a pilot or experiment in one village or town?" I'll get a million arguments, reasons as to why it can't be done. Like "India's too complex", instead of just saying, "Okay, let's give it a try, let's experiment."'

Managing communication in meetings

Here's what Madhav says:

> It is common to have people talk a lot at meetings. When I was in Hong Kong and I had a multicultural team, it was really difficult to get people to speak. Some of the best observations would come from a Japanese or a Chinese guy, but he would speak maybe once in the meeting or once in three meetings! But an Indian has a lot to say! The discussion will keep veering off because a lot of people have a lot to contribute, not necessarily in and around that specific issue but very anecdotally, not very research- or data-led. So you have to keep driving a meeting to a conclusion and you have to say, 'Okay, what's your point? What's the data that you're bringing to the table? What are we trying to solve?' You have to keep bringing that back!

On a lighter note, this habit of wanting to say something even if it's not relevant is sometimes attributed to the practice in management institutes of awarding points based on class participation – a habit that gets ingrained, resulting in people making needless comments in office discussions for the sake of brownie points.

And people don't just talk – they talk with passion and emotion. Susanne, who has been in India since 2014, says: 'People here show emotions – good and bad. I see joy and celebration and laughter all the time. They laugh a lot, but there can also be a lot of angry shouting. There have been a number of occasions when I've had to stop people having a stand-up fight in front of others. The emotion and passion sometimes lead to shouting over other people and not letting others speak.'

Getting the topic back on track takes dexterity and focus. Meetings have to be driven firmly to outcomes. It has to be ensured that the agenda points are discussed. Having an agenda for the time-bound meeting followed by a more fluid open forum helps. If people digress and start rambling, the boss or the meeting organizer has to step in, show authority, ask people to allow everyone to speak, and get them to get back on point.

James says, 'The engagement is great because you get ideas and solutions, but if it becomes a circular discussion, I would cut it before it gets personal or unhealthy and help diffuse the situation.'

Not speaking up

While Indians are talkative and expressive, there is a dichotomy – they don't always speak up or share what they are thinking in difficult situations. Broadly speaking, there is a reticence and unwillingness to stand up for oneself or get into conflicts as Indians don't like to confront.

So, in general, there is more emotion on display at the workplace but dissent is less visible. However, it cannot be said that dissent and disagreement are never expressed. They are, depending on factors like the organizational culture, the hierarchy structure, the temperament of people and how comfortable they are with each other.

Feedback and performance evaluations

Consider this anecdote shared by Rajan:

> When I was in the US, I did an evaluation of a person of Indian origin in my team. So we were doing the yearly appraisal and I shared his areas of improvement. To my surprise, the person gave me a thousand reasons why he didn't agree with it. He made me remove all my comments. He didn't want anything going on his record which would be registered on the organization's HR files. And I was like, 'Listen, if you don't want to improve, it is your loss, not mine! You will stay where you are.'

When I asked my interviewees – expats as well as Indians – about their experience of performance evaluations of Indians, their views had one thing in common: performance evaluations with Indians can be difficult.

Peter remarks, 'In my entire career, the most difficult performance evaluations/pay reviews have been with Indians! Because they largely believe that they are all underpaid, they should have a higher performance rating than they get. They will challenge on pay and seniority but not in terms of anything technical or strategic.'

At the outset, it's relevant to point out that Indians challenging feedback is a phenomenon that occurs more at middle or senior levels and not so much at lower levels. Let's try and understand why Indians challenge feedback when it is negative.

One factor is the huge ambition. People want to make it big in a short time span, one that is often unrealistic. As Anand observes: 'I think that a lot of people outside India struggle with the Indian time frame to succeed. Indians want to conquer the world in three or four years!'

Another factor is that people seem to have a positive view of their achievements, which is not always realistic. Ryan (name changed), a senior executive of an Indo-German insurance start-up, says, 'I would say that the general expectation of achieving a goal is always 'I have achieved', but here the base expectation is that 'I have overachieved'. So there may be clear under-performance, and then to productively communicate that is a challenge!'

And it's taken personally!

In an article in *Bangalore Mirror* on emotions in the Indian workplace, published on 21 April 2016, Kirthiga Reddy, who was Managing Director of Facebook India, said that in the US, Facebook as a company would have things like open peer-to-peer feedback and all information was lateral. 'Building such a culture in India takes a long time. People take things too personally here rather than logically.'

On a similar note, Amit observed that in the US around 20-30 per cent of his time was spent around people issues, whereas in India it went up to about 50 per cent.

Kanchana's experience sums up the factors at play:

> **In person feedback:**
> Feedback sessions are a task in India! I've struggled with Indian managers as I've had to search for what they are trying to tell me

because it's cloaked with so many niceties. They are so conditioned to cushioning the feedback that it loses edge. Strangely, I am looking for direct feedback.

With other cross-cultural global managers, I've never had this issue because they are so direct that sometimes I wished they would be kind!

For instance, I was providing feedback to someone on areas for improvement. I said, 'Here are your three areas of improvement.' I don't know how else to say it! If I want to say, 'You need to be more collaborative,' I am not going to start with why collaboration is important! The person is a responsible professional and should already know that! What good would niceties be if they don't deliver the intended feedback?

Performance appraisals:
Another area is the year-end appraisal, where culturally Indians are so different. Indian colleagues do not value the sanctity nor the objectivity of a year-end appraisal. At appraisals, they talk about their values. A lot of people have told me, 'But I'm honest and frank. I'm very committed. I demonstrate high integrity.' These are hygiene markers in a job! It's about demonstrating these values and making a positive impact for the organization.

People don't comprehend a 'Meets expectations' score. Everybody wants 'Exceeds expectations'. But 'Meets expectations' means that one is good at his job! People take it as an affront to their personality. But I am not talking about *a person* – I am talking about *his performance* for *a* year!

Let's try and understand this from the Indian's perspective. Indians tend to get defensive at performance evaluations, probably more than people from other cultures, perhaps because they feel that they have invested a lot of their time – including hours of personal time – and energy. Also, the fact that they are emotional and work is a huge part of their identity and life are other factors. Simply put, they care and take this seriously, too seriously probably.

Given the above, how have people dealt with this?

What a few people have done, successfully, is to keep it simple: keep it objective, remove the emotion and be constructive. Based on her sixteen years of working with Indians, Virginia states, 'You have to be very sensitive with criticism. Also, I think the Indian male has a very fragile ego; you need to understand that and nurture it a little bit. There should be a lot of positivity surrounding what you are trying to say.'

Here's Kevin's perspective:

> I think one of the things I can do better, as a boss, is to create an appropriate setting for performance feedback. For example, if I want to communicate a message, how do I communicate it so that it's seen as a learning for the team but at the same time I don't embarrass or belittle that person publicly. India has taught me how to be patient. I think the focus is more on how I maintain the self-esteem and confidence of the person or the group of people while giving them feedback.

Lost in Translation: 'Yes I can!'

This is where the rubber meets the road. What is the No. 1 challenge that expats face when working with Indians? The one common issue that came up in my interviews was about people committing and not delivering. Hearing a 'Yes', which should usually be a good thing as opposed to disagreement, seems to be, ironically, the single biggest challenge or source of frustration amongst expats and repatriates.

David shares his experience:

> This affirmative attitude of an Indian mind is not necessarily a commitment one can count on the following day as well. I had started with my Indian team here an initiative to clean up in the factory. Everybody wanted to support and do it but finally, when it was time to do something, almost nobody appeared. So it's a 'Yes' and then, when we have to implement, sometimes it's a different story!

People easily say 'Yes' if you ask them 'Can you do this?' When asked if this can be done by next week – an unrealistic date – the answer will still be 'Yes'. And when the task they agreed to do is not done, people make excuses. This is very annoying to people from other cultures. They would like an honest answer based on a realistic assessment – not a 'Yes', which pleases them in the short term, only to doubly upset them in the long term.

Stans says:

> The biggest difference between working in India and overseas is that people here don't necessarily tell you what's on their mind. In the West, if asked a question like 'Can you deliver this?', you say 'Yes' or 'No'. Or you will say, 'I can do it by next week.' In India, when I ask someone, 'Can you do it?', the answer is always 'Yes'. If I make the mistake of saying, 'I need it by a certain date', they will say 'Yes'. And the day before the deadline, they will say, 'The sky has fallen, or there were floods or electricity breakdowns, or the monsoon caused chaos, or they had a family emergency!'

Given that this is a big cause of frustration, let's try and understand the reasons for this behaviour. The first reason is conditioning. Many Indians have lived in joint or extended families, where they grew up acquiescing to requests and instructions from elders, and saying 'Yes' was common. So it's very likely that saying 'Yes' may be the first thing that comes to mind for a lot of people. It's almost like a reflex.

While Indians may be direct at times, they are reluctant to say 'No' possibly due to the value placed on saving face. It's almost like: 'You are my friend or long-term client – I don't want to disappoint you up front, so I agree because it's the easy or right thing to do.'

Another factor to bear in mind is the Indian approach to time – and timelines. It can sometimes be casual, and there is a tendency to commit to a deadline without taking into account whether the task is in fact doable in that time.

A related factor is that people mean to do the job, but then are not able to do so due to poor planning and prioritization. In India, hope is a big factor; the person is hopeful that somehow it will happen because his intentions are noble. Sometimes it's also because of an overestimation of one's abilities. The attitude is 'Of course I can do this', and the details can be worked out and worried about later. People often don't weigh their words carefully.

Saying 'Yes' and not delivering may also be the effect of how motivated the employee is, or how much 'buy-in' he has to do the particular task. Also, at times, there could be a miscommunication or disconnect because the person didn't understand the job or what it entailed but didn't express his concerns.

Do problems or 'bad news' get escalated?

Something that compounds and complicates the matter is the communication of bad news. If, after commencing work on the task or project, there is a problem that impacts its implementation or outcome, the boss would like to know about it as soon as possible. This doesn't happen, at least easily, in India. People tell you what they think you would want to hear. So the good news is shared but the bad news is underplayed or not shared. People probably hope that the problem will get resolved soon or somehow disappear! Peter says:

> I do get a sense from the Indian staff that they like to say things like, 'Oh, everything's fine, don't worry. I'm on top of it, I'll deal with it.' There's quite a bit of that. I think a lot of this (behaviour) is cultural. People don't want to give you bad news; they will always put a positive spin on almost everything.

In a lighter vein, Sateen says, 'Because people don't ask or approach you, you don't know whether you are in trouble. They feel, "The boss is there to beat me up." By the time things go so badly, the boss can't do anything but beat them up!'

Rajesh explains this well:

> In general, people in India are driven. They want results and they will genuinely try and do things, notwithstanding the poor performers. But people here think that if they face a problem, or if they get stuck, they can rationalize it and explain that it didn't happen due to x, y, z reasons. They assume that you will cut them some slack when they have genuinely tried, gone 50 per cent of

> the way and then hit a roadblock. The thinking is, 'It's not that I didn't mean to do it, I did try doing the job.'

Often one finds that while there may be communication gaps when it comes to the problem, communication is not lacking when it comes to giving explanations or excuses!

Does this happen only in India?

One implication of working around the above is having to follow up with people, as discussed later. But let's consider: Is not saying 'No' and having to follow up with people unique to India? Do people from other countries always deliver when they say they will?

With regard to following up, Amit, who studied and worked in the US for twenty years before coming to India, makes an interesting observation. He says, 'There are small sections in the US with whom you have to follow up. I would say 80 per cent of the people in the US meet their commitments, and with 20 per cent you have to follow up. In India it's the reverse.'

According to an expat who has lived in different places: 'Thailand is pretty good with delivering as per timelines. In Jakarta, you have to do quite a lot of following up. That's also the case in the UK. You have to follow up everywhere these days.'

As regards not saying 'No', this is not unique to India as people who have lived in other Asian countries can corroborate. Amy agrees. She says that she has experienced this in South Korea and Myanmar too.

Yuk Dong Kim, former CEO, Shinhan Bank, says, 'When I was working in Japan too, Japanese people didn't say "No" directly. If they said "Please let me think", it usually meant "No"!'

In her insightful book, *The Culture Map: Breaking Through the Invisible Boundaries of Global Business,* Erin Meyer points out that saying 'No' between the lines is common throughout Asia, including China, Japan and Korea, especially when speaking to a boss or a client. One will discover that 'No' can come in many guises like a sharp sucking in of breath or a non-committal answer such as, 'It will be very difficult but I'll do my best,' or, 'We'll think about it.'

To sum up, while not saying 'No' and having to follow up with people is not unique to India, it is prevalent and may be more pronounced here. It's relevant to mention here that how a person experiences this communication nuance in India also depends on his frame of reference. A person who has not worked in a less developed country will find it challenging to work around this aspect, as compared to someone who has worked in one.

So, how does the manager work around the 'Yes'?

Listed below are a few things that managers have tried out:

Check-ins

Most bosses find that frequent check-ins to monitor progress work well. Joe says, 'Nothing's done unless it's done and even then it's not done! The need to follow up is there. You can't give directions and leave it. You need to have a strong reminder system.'

It's like saying, 'I trust you but I need to validate.'

Amit elaborates on this: 'There are two sets of people in India: the top tier which is talented, committed, smart, hard-working, delivers when they commit and they run on their own. The other set is competitive but a bit sloppy, commits but doesn't deliver or follow up on their commitment, they are ambitious and think of the next job, not the job at hand. There are two things I did to work with the second set. One, I had very clearly defined outcomes or measures. There was no ambiguity around the timeline attached. Two, I would check on them frequently.'

Check that the timelines are realistic

Most projects are planned around deliverables; key milestones are defined with the employee concerned, and tracked. But sometimes the timelines that are set are unrealistic to begin with.

Ryan says, 'This kind of living in denial starts with setting a timeline. You ask, "How long do we need for this?" and the person may say, "Four months." And you know that four months looks difficult but you say, "Let's work with four months." You do a little project planning, you set milestones, and after the first month or second month, if you are really far behind and everyone is relaxed, that's living in denial because you are not going to be able to meet that deadline given the resources. How do you manage? It's either by escalating or often it's by throwing more resources at the project at the last minute to get it sorted out, and quite a few times it's by extending the timeline. I feel shifting timelines is much easier in India than in other places.'

It's important to align and agree with the person or the team as to what is a realistic timeline. A good way of confirming the person's ability to do the task is to ask open-ended clarifying questions. Josh, who has been working in India for three years, says, 'You have to openly communicate. I would say things like "Tell me what you understand of this" to figure out whether we were on the same page.'

Stans offers this viewpoint:

Learn how to ask the right questions, so you get the answers you need. In my previous job, I had to deal a lot with people in India. I would ask more questions and not assume as much as one would in the West. I learned to ask, 'So when can you do it?' or 'What other projects do you have on your plate?' or 'Can I call on Wednesday to get a status update?'

Reading verbal and non-verbal communication

People may not say 'No' directly but they often communicate it in other ways. If a person from a more direct culture is asked on a Friday to submit something on Monday, he might say, 'Sorry, it's my weekend.' The Indian who doesn't want to do the task over the weekend may not say so directly but will find a different way of letting you know that he would rather not do it. For example, he may look down or look away or talk in a softer, unconvincing tone or reply in monosyllables.

Sudhir and Katharina Kakar, in their 2009 book *The Indians: Portrait of a People*, articulate this well when they say, 'With the preservation of relationships as the primary principle governing their actions in interpersonal situations, Indians find it difficult to say a frank 'No' to requests they are unable or unwilling to grant. The refusal has then to be interpreted from the words in which the rejection is couched ("Let's see") or ("It's difficult but I will try" and so on), and from the tentative tone of voice and cautious body language.'

Indian bosses have an advantage here, in that, they can read body language and determine, to some extent, the readiness of the person to do the job. Some expats I interviewed had also learnt to read between the lines. Ryan says, 'It's something one has to get a sense of from just living here and interacting with people.' Another says, 'Reading the "yes" is sometimes difficult, but you get a feeling for it.' And, I'd like to add here, when in doubt, always clarify.

Building in buffers

Another thing that may work, and which is implemented by some, is setting a deadline a few days ahead of the actual one. They build in a buffer so that even if there is a delay, the final deadline would still be met.

Documenting decisions and follow-up actions

This has worked for some like Craig, who says:

> Often you leave an office feeling that you've agreed to something, and then something very different or perhaps nothing happens. One of the things that I have instituted (at ASB) is that we close every conversation with a corporate by simply saying, 'Let me just share with you what I've captured.' I read the points that we have agreed to and say, 'Did I miss anything?' and 'Okay, so I will send an email to you in an hour with all of this.' And in the email I will say, 'If I have anything wrong, please respond. If I don't hear from you, I am assuming we are on the same page.'
>
> And I notice that the person responds soon because if he does not write back, there is a trail. And while this approach has made a lot of people uncomfortable, it has enabled more transparency. People now give me a more realistic time frame.

Building trust

Last but definitely not the least, trust is an important constituent of the workplace dynamics as discussed in an earlier chapter.

Given below are a few examples of effective communication strategies that people have used to much success.

The experience of a European executive:

> Dealing with complex situations at work requires a combination of experience, intuition, empathy and leadership skills. Because in certain situations, you are going to say, 'That's the way we are going to do it whether you like it or not and I will control the implementation.' In other situations, you may say, 'Don't tell me such non-truths, now tell me the truth behind this.' And I think it's very important to establish a level of trust. Because, if the employees don't trust you as the manager of the company, you will never get the full truth.
>
> So I hired people in a way that they would be capable of saying 'No'. We hired a CFO and an HR person who had previous experience with Western companies. I tried to identify and encourage their ability to be crystal-clear and give a counter-argument. When I was sitting at telephone conferences, I would press the mute button and I would say, 'Now, say "No" to the CEO in Europe.' They learnt to make a good argument, give explanations and bring their points to the table in a very good way.

Anand suggests the following:

> The first thing a manager has to do is make his direct reports feel comfortable. He needs to set his agenda and talk about his management style. One of the things he should mention is that he has to be the *first* person to get to know bad news. And he has to reassure them that there is no shame in asking for help.

The other thing that has to be established up front is the credit piece. The desire to succeed and to get ahead leads to a lot of people wanting to take credit; on the flip side, a lot of people are afraid to accept accountability if things don't go to plan. Make sure you establish how you will share credit and work through rewards.

Make sure that there is a process for raising flags and that there is in place a more formal project execution team. So when you build a team, you need to have someone who has gone through all that, who is a little ahead on that curve so that they make sure that deadlines are met. And India is getting better at this.

Conclusion

As can be seen, communication is anything but simple in India! There are various nuances, and while one can't dwell on all of them, hopefully the important ones have been fleshed out here.

In general – and also given the reluctance to decide, commit and be accountable – it may not be easy to work around these nuances. Accountability cannot be assumed; it has to be articulated and driven. Expectations have to be clarified and reinforced. There is a need to follow up, the degree or extent of which depends on the drive, capability, track record and experience of the individual to whom the task is given.

Ultimately, implementation is to a large extent dependent on leaders and their ability to articulate clear, specific and tangible deliverables. The boss has to put in place a transparent system, where there are periodic check-ins and everybody knows what's expected. A culture of openness and comfort will go a long way in ensuring that everyone is on the same page.

5

Two Minutes!

*A*rvind was on cloud nine.

Twenty-eight years old, two years into his first job in Mumbai as a research analyst, and his boss Sanjay asks him if he would like to take up a lateral job vacancy and move to Singapore. He asks him to think about it and get back.

What's there to think about? He is: Single. Young. Mobile. Ambitious. No more crazy commuting and spending maddeningly long hours at work in Mumbai. A comfortable, clean city with tropical climate that isn't too far away from home. Singapore, it is.

Fast forward two months: It's Arvind's first week in Singapore. He has been scouting for houses and has shortlisted a few apartments close to his office. This morning he has an important meeting with a pharmaceutical company that his firm has been researching on from an investment viewpoint for a while. Sanjay and Arvind are slated to meet with the CEO and the CFO of the client company, let's call it Tonedo Pharma.

The meeting is scheduled at 9 a.m. at Tonedo's office at Raffles Place, one of Singapore's business districts. At 8.55 a.m. Sanjay enters the client's office and is ushered into the meeting room where the clients are already seated. There is no sign of Arvind. Five minutes go by, then ten. Initial pleasantries have been made and they are about to discuss the business at hand. Sanjay keeps glancing at his cellphone, which has just flashed a message from Arvind saying, 'Almost there'. Another seven minutes pass by, and there is still no sign of him when, at 9.23 a.m., Arvind walks in with a flourish and says, 'Sorry, the train was late.' There is a stunned, absolute silence. Sanjay uncomfortably shuffles his feet and discreetly looks away, embarrassed. Late train? This is Singapore!

One quick takeaway: Old habits die hard. One can always blame the traffic or trains in India when one is delayed! But not everywhere around the world.

Before we discuss how time is viewed in India, let's understand it first from a broader perspective.

Different approaches to time

Anthropologist Edward T. Hall has explored how different cultures – monochronic and polychronic – deal with time. A monochronic culture structures various activities based on a linear notion of time. This culture has a rigid approach to time and focuses on 'getting the job done'. Time is scheduled, arranged and managed. A polychronic culture structures various activities based on interpersonal relationships with people and views time as cyclic and relative. This culture has a flexible approach to time and focuses on relationships; several things can be done simultaneously.

Germany, Switzerland, the US, UK and Canada are some countries that are monochronic. As are Japan and South Korea. The Philippines, Mexico, Indonesia and Saudi Arabia are examples of countries that are polychronic. Indians, for the most part, have a polychronic approach to time.

In a lighter vein, Justin says: 'In India, time is more elastic, so ten minutes means 'Whatever'. But there are lots of countries where that's the case like Spain, Thailand, Italy, where ten minutes means an hour or whatever. In most hot countries in the Pacific, you have that! For some reason hot weather makes people more laid-back with their timekeeping. You don't tend to get that in colder countries; that's just my theory!'

In general, time is loosely interpreted in India. That said, not all Indians have flexible notions of time. Raised as I have been by parents who value time to a fault, I can relate to the sense of frustration when people don't turn up on time. I have come across people who think it's perfectly acceptable to be late, whether it's to work or to a dinner. And I have seen people, from all walks of life, who are always punctual. However, in general, the broad societal trend is of not being very particular about time. Given this and the fact that time has an impact on work, communication and lifestyle, working with and around this approach to time is, and can be, one of the biggest challenges in India.

In this chapter we look at the way Indians view time, and discuss a few factors that may explain why they view it the way they do. We also look at how people, Indians and non-Indians, have dealt with time issues. Hopefully, this discussion would facilitate some understanding around this aspect – and help in alleviating some stress!

The Indian approach to time

I spoke with Chloe, who moved to India a few years ago with her husband Nick. Her father is Indian and mother American. This is what she shares about her growing-up years:

When I think of things that I wasn't really used to in India, a huge one is the concept of time. When I started working here, I noticed that things got done later than I had asked for – sometimes by a few hours. But then it kind of reminded me of growing up in the US. My dad worked a lot, but in my mom's world, he was always late! My mom would ask him to do something and he would get it done but not at the time she expected it to be done. In my house, my mom would set the clocks fifteen minutes ahead. I always wondered why we did that, and I think it was for my dad's sake!

It is commonly acknowledged that Indians move to a different time zone, jokingly referred to as Indian Stretchable Time. Let's try and understand a few reasons underlying this.

Priorities are different

It's relevant to point out that the value of time is often not instilled in many Indian homes and families. Even if it is by words, it is seldom reinforced by actions! This may be a function of one's education, exposure or other factors. As Parag points out, 'It's a reflection of the level of sophistication of our society.' People who have experienced its value and importance may have a different approach to it than those who haven't.

For many people in the Western – and Eastern – world, time is sacrosanct. People take appointments seriously, with a view to honouring them regardless of what else may come up in their personal or social life. The priority is to respect someone's time and, in doing so, to respect the person they are interacting with.

When I was working in a multicultural organization in Singapore, I observed that with people from other cultures, if one is not on time or does not deliver on time, that is an indication of one's professionalism or, rather, the lack of it. Whereas in India, this is not necessarily how it is perceived. Also, in India, the relationship is often prioritized over work and, in doing so, if time is not adhered to, so be it. Of course, this is not always the case professionally but it is something that comes into play often enough.

Nick and Chloe share this perceptive observation:

> I think concepts of time are very different in India because priorities are very different. In the US if you are late, you better have a good excuse. And in India, it is, 'Something else came up.' It's a matter of priorities. It doesn't have to be, 'I was in the hospital' or 'My wife was dying'. It could be, 'Somebody needed help, so I gave it to them.'

Inefficient infrastructure

Even with the most earnest intentions of being on time for a meeting in India, it must be said that you are often fighting against odds. There are several external factors that can render you – and the people you meet – late for a meeting. For instance, traffic, which is unpredictable. It may take twenty minutes to reach some place on a normal day and suddenly you have a protest march or the roads may be dug up and the same distance can now take an hour! Traffic may be stopped to make way for a senior minister or the local trains may be delayed.

People who have lived and worked in the West and, closer home, in countries like Singapore, Hong Kong and Japan, where one can predict travel times fairly accurately, find that these efficiencies are lacking in a developing country like India.

Virginia puts it well when she says, 'I think the main difference between working in India and more developed countries is the infrastructure. Not having that infrastructure here slows you down and stops all of us from being the best that we can be.'

Time is cyclical

Religion may be a factor in shaping the way some people perceive time.

In Hinduism, time is cyclical, with there being no definite beginning and end. Also, there is the belief that one cannot control external factors. This may explain why people are accommodating when others are late; by the same yardstick, they expect that they should be cut some slack in similar situations!

Approach to time at work

The above said, let's consider how the approach to time is manifested in the workplace.

The Indian day

Due to factors like distances and long commutes to work, it's normal for people to reach office around 9 a.m. or later. People leave office late, reach home late and the next day it's the same cycle all over. So the Indian day starts and ends later than in many other places in Asia and the world.

Justin elaborates on this: 'Indians tend to go to bed a lot later than people in the West. Most people in our country tend to be in bed by 10 or 10.30 p.m., whereas in India they are probably eating dinner then! And their day tends to start later. Here, we have staff coming in and having their breakfast at work!'

Keeping to appointments

Over the years, I have observed that people from linear cultures readily commit to appointments even if they are three or four weeks away – and actually keep to them. Initially, I was amazed to find that a call with a colleague or a client that was mutually agreed to many days previously takes place without any reminders, at exactly the scheduled time!

This quality or tendency I have seen sparingly in Indians. One possible reason for this, as highlighted by Madhav, is that people tend not to have too much visibility of their calendars. He says, 'When you take an appointment, if it's within the next three or four days, people have visibility of their calendars. But not beyond that. They will agree to a meeting one month down the line and then, as you get closer to the date, it will get cancelled. So the culture of appointments is very different.'

Martin Bienz, Consul General of Switzerland, says, 'A related matter is that when we have events and we send out invitations, people do not RSVP immediately. People from the Diplomatic Corps and some Indians confirm on time, but very often we don't get RSVPs from many of our Indian guests. So my staff has to follow up with calls to the invitees closer to the date of the event. Another tendency is of people not turning up, despite confirming their attendance, because something else comes up. Earlier we used to send out our invitations a month before an event so that they have enough time to plan, but people don't commit one month in advance, so now we send the invites two weeks prior to the event.'

Internal meetings

As to whether internal meetings begin on time, this depends on the type of organization, the organizational culture and the working style of the meeting organizer. Usually, in professional organizations, meetings start on time – more or less!

Meetings in India may not always have an agenda. If they do, it may not be adhered to. This, and tendencies like making small talk, result in meetings going on longer than they should.

Also, Indians are accustomed to doing things simultaneously, like signing papers or even taking urgent calls during meetings. One should not infer from these behaviours a lack of interest or attention (although that may be the case at times). They are often a function of people operating under constraints and demands unique to the Indian context.

External and client meetings

While external meetings often take place on time, that may not be the case where an external service provider like a consultant is scheduled to meet a client.

Amit remarks, 'Clients don't care; in fact, it is common practice to make you wait. We went to Delhi to meet a director of a prominent organization and he kept us waiting for two and a half hours. I just got up, wrote on the back of my business card that we were waiting, kept it on his table and left.'

Eric has a similar view: 'I travel all over India to meet clients. I will often have a three o'clock meeting which starts at six o'clock. So you have to be careful with the flights, keep a big margin and honestly it's a huge waste of time.'

Not only do clients make one wait, but they may also take one's time for granted in other ways. Madhav shares his experience:

The nature of client meetings is very different in India. When you work abroad and come back, you're used to a very structured, appointment-based working style and you organize your day around that. When you take over a new role, some clients just call you and drop in for tea or because they were in the neighbourhood.

This doesn't happen with all clients; with some clients, it can be an ad hoc thing. The agenda will come up in the meeting. And you may have something going on such as an international video conference to participate in, but obviously if a client has turned up, you go and meet him.

Time adherence in corporate India

This is what some people had to say about their experiences and observations of Indians and time.

'Zero value for time saved,' says an Indian executive:

Our organization builds toll roads. The world over, consultants place a value on the time saved in determining toll levels. In India, that is a recipe for disaster. It turns out that the Indian commuter places a value of zero on time saved!

Let me elucidate with an example: the owner of a manufacturing unit, located off one of our toll roads, drove to work every morning in a spanking new Mercedes. That car must have cost him a pretty packet. Yet, he always took the toll-free service road that ran alongside the toll road even though it took him longer and caused more wear and tear. The Rs 30 toll was just too much for him to bear! This is only an example but typical of the mindset!

'It's getting better,' according to a German expat:

> You have huge differences between north, west and south of India. So, Mumbai, compared to six years ago, is getting a lot better. If people come fifteen minutes late to a meeting, they actually excuse themselves. In the past, they would come in forty minutes late and it was always the traffic. You still get that as an excuse but it's a lot better!

'Efficient but...' says an Australian teacher who has worked in five countries:

> The way I describe India to everybody is that it's a place of diametrically opposite everything. Anything that you can envision about a place/people, it exists here, as does its polar opposite. For example, the network administrators at the school are very efficient. They literally have a five-minute response time. But then there are people who turn up late by hours!

'It's been good' for a European executive:

> Actually people laugh at me when I say that, at work, I find people extremely punctual! I've had several meetings in different cities but very few where people showed up late. Traffic is a challenge in cities everywhere, whether it's us going to a meeting or other people meeting us. Despite that, I have to say that people have been extremely punctual. In the office too, people show up on time. They often work through lunch and leave late.
>
> A common perception is that people cancel meetings at the last minute. We've had some of those, and my colleague will say, 'Oh, typical India.' And I say, 'Don't say that too quickly because

in the US, you have the same thing. If people don't want to talk to you, they often cancel at the last minute with some excuse.' It's really not that different.

As one can see, punctuality standards differ across organizations and people. One can expect to have a range of experiences when it comes to time adherence in the corporate world in India!

The two-minute syndrome

Growing up, a favourite snack for my generation (incidentally, also for my daughter's generation) was Maggi noodles. They were tasty, simple and easy to make. But their USP was encapsulated in the mother in the advertisement telling her kids to wait for just 'two minutes'. Unlike most other Indian home-made snacks that took considerably longer to make, here was instant gratification in a pack. The point to note here is that the noodles rarely took just 'two minutes' to prepare.

While this book does not cover issues relating to day-to-day living in India, it's relevant to mention the attitude towards time amongst the less educated and in the unorganized sector. As with Maggi, it is a common practice for people to tell others who are waiting for them that they will arrive in 'two minutes'. Needless to say, this does not mean two minutes literally, but that they intend to be there 'soon'. This behaviour can cause a lot of frustration as it keeps the other person waiting, sometimes for hours! And if they can't make it, often they don't inform the person who is expecting them.

But there is a dichotomy with regard to time in the social sphere: while people are often late by hours otherwise, they observe time to the minute for special or religious occasions. For example, Indian weddings have ceremonies that begin at auspicious times and these can be as precise as 10.14 a.m. or 3.47 p.m.

How have people worked around time-related issues at work?

While it is difficult initially to deal with punctuality and related issues, as people settle in, they find ways of working around them. However, more often than not, it should be kept in mind that there is no solution!

Chris remarks: 'Everybody is in a hurry, trying to push their way through, yet no one seems to turn up for meetings on time. To help my managers understand the value of time and the importance of turning up for meetings on time, I used to start by quoting the cost of the meeting to stress on the value we needed to get out of it, and I resorted to fining people for being late. I allowed them five grace minutes. After that, for every five minutes they were fined Rs 100, with the money going to charity.'

Joe, who found that there wasn't much punctuality when he took over, made the latecomer sing, dance or tell a joke! After the first time he did this, no one was late again!

Monitoring or punitive measures may not go down well with people. That said, discipline in some form, shape or manner may need to be driven. When it comes to getting people on time to internal meetings, the boss, in a hierarchical culture like India, sets the tone and expectations. If people know that the boss means business and expects everyone to be on time for meetings, they may be late a few times but eventually they will get the message.

Brendon's advice is worth noting: 'I think terminology and meanings need to be clarified. And what time means to me and what time means to you!'

Sateen, usually mild-mannered, says, 'You've got to shake things up. If people didn't show up for fifteen minutes, I would go away.'

Richard van der Merwe tried a different tack to instil respect for time in his organization:

> The first couple of townhalls that I had with the staff here started fifteen or twenty minutes late. For the next one, I arrived twenty minutes before it started at 3 p.m. I handed out a sealed card and a wrapped gift to everybody who arrived on time. At three o' clock sharp, I stopped giving these. The others who came late looked at the people who had the cards and gifts and asked, 'What happened?' You will not believe how well this worked! The card had a simple message: 'Dear colleague, you have shown respect for others, you are regarded as reliable, thank you for being on time.'

In Hari's organization, this is what they implemented with great success: 'We solved the punctuality problem by implementing a rule that whoever came late for a meeting had to buy a shirt for all those kept waiting! I still recall when a senior colleague, on his first day at work, came some two seconds late for a meeting. There were twenty of us in that meeting and he had to buy twenty shirts! As you can imagine, our on-time performance has been impeccable ever since!'

Ultimately, in order to work across cultures, acceptance of the good and the bad is an important prerequisite for success. One can complain incessantly and find fault, but eventually it's the people who realize that 'this is the way it is' and work around it are the ones who are successful.

Amy Sebes, who has lived in seven countries including India, puts things in perspective:

In India I find that if someone says to me, 'I'll be there in five minutes,' it doesn't mean five minutes! To me, it means, 'I'll be there as soon as I can; it may be an hour but my intent is to come.' So it's that view of time.

In Germany, 8 p.m. means exactly 8 p.m. If you are early to someone's house, you wait at the front door until it's 8 and then you ring the door bell. In India, when someone invites us over to their house at 8 p.m., being American, we show up at 8. But here 8 can mean 7.45 or 9.30.

Regarding how I deal with it, I just keep in mind that this is a place where time is viewed differently and I can't change how other people are! I just accept it.

Way of working: deadlines and dates

While on the topic of time, it's relevant to dwell a bit on the way people work with regard to deadlines.

According to Joe, 'The job gets done at the end of the day but the planning is poor, the process isn't structured and a lot of the work happens at the last minute.'

Less planning and process

In general, working in India is less structured. As mentioned earlier, processes aren't always robust or streamlined.

Ryan says, 'In my country, in case of a social event, the week before everything would be organized, probably structured with a project plan. And here it's three in the afternoon, nothing is standing, nothing is ready, but by evening you have this grand set-up standing, thanks to the huge number of people who have been thrown into the project!'

People don't necessarily plan ahead or work with the plan. Also, there's less of anticipating what might happen or thinking through consequences. It's more of 'take it as it comes'.

Eric says, 'I am managing the operation and the maintenance of the metro in Mumbai. We have to plan the maintenance for thirty years. It's almost impossible to convince our client about something like that! In general, it is unconceivable here how to plan for such a long time. I force my team to plan, I explain to them the result and why we plan. We put in place some processes, knowing that it will be good for the future. It may make no difference on a day-to-day basis, but after five or ten years it will be very good.'

Related to the above point, 'It's done differently,' says Susanne:

> Our organization is renowned for delivering very big projects and it does that very effectively. But it's done differently from what I have been used to. Things do get delivered, and normally on time and on budget, but the way it's done is very different. It will depend on calling in favours from people because there's a strong bond and relationship there. And everyone pulling in together at the last minute to get things done.
>
> I don't see much of planning and setting goals and thinking through not just milestones and actions but also what risks might come up, what things might destabilize us and what we would do if that happened. Despite that, however, things get delivered!

Working last minute

In India, creating a shared sense of urgency in the team can be a challenge. Rajan says, 'Unless you make people understand how important the date is, deadlines and dates don't mean much. They can keep moving.'

In a lighter vein, Sateen says, 'Eighty per cent of the work gets done in the last twenty per cent of time!'

'It's not that people are lazy. There is a high tendency to procrastinate but then people may work all night or through the weekend. People do things in bursts,' observes James.

But the Indian approach to time is not always a negative!

Is there an upside to the Indian approach to time? Surprisingly, yes. One finds that Indians are more flexible.

As Madhav points out, 'People are very accommodating if you land up half an hour late, and they expect you to be accommodating if they land up half an hour late!'

If it's possible to do so, they are open to juggling their calendar and making changes. Also, Indians are more flexible about working longer hours or working on holidays.

Craig says, 'With my Indian staff, seventeen different things may be scheduled for a Wednesday and they will manage it. They will work all night long and up to the last minute and do whatever it takes to deliver.'

If a deadline is not being met, they will stretch themselves and try to make things happen. As Chris points out, 'One thing that is common across the globe is people's ability and willingness to step up in the event of a crisis, but in India that was even more evident. We always got the job done. If we had a bandh in Bangalore, people would come early morning before the bandh came into effect for their shift which didn't start until noon – that's the level of commitment here. When you need them to, people go well beyond the call of duty.'

This is put in perspective by Erin Meyer in an article in the *Harvard Business Review*, titled 'The Cultural Perils of Clockwatching'. She says that while people in every culture want one to be both structured and flexible, some cultures such as the German, Dutch, British, Danish, Australian and American tend to value structure over flexibility. 'But,' she goes on to say, 'in many of the world's fastest-growing countries, such as Brazil, India, Indonesia, Russia and Nigeria, there is much more emphasis put on being flexible than on being structured. In these cultures, strongly emphasizing punctuality signals an inability to adapt and even a lack of priorities.'

Conclusion

In India, appointments and times are often approximate and could be viewed more as a time frame than an actual time on the clock. This said, if one is meeting people from professional organizations, appointments are usually on time.

Broadly speaking, time adherence in India can be one of the bigger challenges for a non-Indian and there is no quick or easy solution to this. A person who places a huge value on appointments and schedules and getting the job done may consider people who do not share a similar regard for time as disrespectful. Given this gap in expectations and mindset, it's worth noting that people in India don't necessarily mean to be disrespectful of others' time. They look at it through their own lens.

In conclusion, here's an anecdote narrated by Martin Bienz: 'I once hosted a social event at my residence and invited about sixty people. It was supposed to start at 7.30 p.m. and the Swiss ambassador was also present. Given the usual practice, we expected people to arrive at 8 or 8.30. To our pleasant surprise, people started arriving before 7.30. Within ten or fifteen minutes, almost everybody who was invited was there!'

Just when one has written off Indians and their sense of time, one could be pleasantly surprised!

6

One Plus Two Equals Four

Ram Lakhan, a popular Hindi film of the 1980s, had a hit song that went '*My name is Lakhan, one, two ka four*'. Colloquially, the last bit is a reference to how things are done in India, and that is what this chapter is about.

Some capabilities of Indians have been shaped by the environment – physical, economic and business. The chaos and complexity offer real-life lessons in how to cope; they equip Indians with the skills required to survive and thrive in difficult situations. Here, I flesh out some of these skills and instincts that hold them in good stead in the corporate world. However, these skills go hand in hand with some less palatable ones, which I will also look at.

Dealing with ambiguity and uncertainty

In general, Indians are good at navigating their way in unclear, nebulous territory. This is a cultural trait that is common to many Indians, given the unpredictable environment in which variables can change at a moment's notice. One cannot assume that yesterday's landscape will necessarily hold true today.

The external environment is dynamic; there can be changes in infrastructure, government regulations and other factors that impact business.

Indians *can* deal with last-minute changes, things not going to plan or breaking down. They do not get bogged down too easily and, in the midst of challenges, they can improvise and get their act together.

In the words of an interviewee: 'I think people here are superbly gifted and are able to deal with ambiguity, which means that they are very quick in adapting to new situations, new challenges, new jobs and new tasks that they are given.'

Madhav elaborates on this: 'People can generally deal with ambiguity, unlike in the West or even in the East in places like Hong Kong. When you are dealing with someone who is Chinese or Korean, you have to give very specific, precise directions. You can't leave it nebulous and expect them to do it because they would like to stick to a script. Whereas here you give broad directions and people can go and execute the task. They actually thrive on something like that. In an ambiguous kind of scenario, they bring in their own creativity.'

Amy shares her views on how Indians' approach to religion and life ties in with this: 'I feel that some of the ability to deal with ambiguity must come from Hinduism, because there's so much of good and bad all together. And Westerners think, "Oh is this a good goddess or a bad goddess?" because it's one or the other for them. But in India it's much more complicated and all good and bad is tied together like no other place I have been to!'

But not everybody thinks or agrees that Indians can deal with ambiguity. After five years in India, Rory, an international school teacher, has realized that when giving instructions, they have to be crystal clear. 'There's no questioning, there's no critical thinking or demonstration of initiative. One thing I find in India is that the leadership is so hierarchical. You start at the top but the critical thinking, initiative and innovation wane as you go down the hierarchy until they almost completely disappear.'

Another factor responsible for this is the education system that doesn't inculcate these skills. A lot of the time, it's 'follow what's told' and 'copy-paste'. On a similar note, Jos says: 'Often, unquestionable, clear instructions need to be given. If something deviates from the straight path, everything tends to stop, and often without reporting, till the boss asks what the status is. At the higher levels, people can work more independently.'

In general, at the lower end of a hierarchical set-up, Indians may be less prone to being proactive and operating well without clarity. They may prefer to be instructed as they are comfortable with and used to following instructions. But at higher levels people are fairly good at navigating ambiguous situations. Broadly speaking, though, there's no denying that Indians can cope with and thrive in ambiguity better than most people.

Sangeeta, who heads human resources for a multinational company, elaborates on the Indian's unique approach and how it translates to professional success:

Indians are used to working and can operate beautifully in greys. Whereas in any other country, people will love black and white. We can deal with ambiguity, that's our strength. If you look at all over Asia, many of the corporate leadership roles are occupied by Indians. Why? Because we come from a market that has taught us to think on our feet, think smart and act on the reflex. We are not in predictable environments. Our ability to navigate and find solutions is probably due to the way our market is and we are taught to fight for ourselves.

I had a team of Singaporeans who would look to the leader for clarity – I want this black and this white. Whereas an Indian team member would find his own way out. He would come back and say, 'I faced this, I did this, I hope that was okay,' versus a person who says, 'I am stuck here, tell me what to do.'

Indians are flexible – and not just with time

As Sven observes metaphorically: 'While planning a project, Indians start walking and the plan will progress along the way. For them it is important to have a good idea about the end point and keep the direction right during the journey. Europeans will be more structured. They will first have the plan in place and then start walking. For them it is important to define up front both the path as well as the end point of the journey. Indians are more flexible in changing plans or in handling unforeseen situations.'

Indians are used to working and interacting with people from different parts of the country having diverse socio-economic backgrounds, religions, beliefs and values. They live and breathe diversity in all its shades and hues and this probably facilitates their ability to accommodate and adapt within and outside India.

Rajan shares his insights: 'One of the key strengths that we possess as Indians is the ability to adapt. To me this is the single most important quality as we travel within India or across the globe on work. The ability to adapt in different countries with extremely different cultures, weather and geography is quite commendable.'

On a lighter note, what most Indians are not very flexible about are their food habits. They tend to be rather fastidious about their food preferences and look to eat dal-chawal or roti-subzi in the remotest corner of the world!

'But in business,' Eric says, 'they are able to take huge financial risks to develop what they think is good for the future. Much more than what we are able to do in France, for example.'

Enterprising

And Indians are nimble. They have a 'Yes, can do' mindset. They may not take into account all the factors or think through the consequences, but they can move quickly and seize opportunities. They have the ability to think on their feet and navigate difficult situations.

I came across an example of this during the demonetization drive in November 2016. After the announcement of phasing out of old notes, people all over the country were standing in long queues to deposit their old currency and withdraw new currency notes from banks. Sometimes, they had to stand in queues for four or five hours.

A news report on TV showed how one proprietor had spotted an opportunity in this situation and offered an innovative and easy solution. Before demonetization, his venture provided helpers on hire to assist with domestic duties like cleaning, grocery shopping, house parties, etc. Given the need of the hour, he extended the scope of his activities – his helpers were now available to stand in queues for people who wanted to withdraw money. When the helpers reached inside the bank, the clients would take their place.

Indians are enterprising. Craig remarks, 'Indians have this inherent business savvy.'

It is widely accepted that certain communities in India have a strong business sense. For example, the Marwaris and Gujaratis are said to be shrewd and street-smart. They have an innate knack for business and have 'business in their blood' as it were. They have a large presence in the lucrative diamond and jewellery, real estate, trading and financial businesses, among others.

Let's consider the case of my local grocer. In the face of competition from bigger and better organized players, many of whom have an online presence, he tries hard to retain his share of the pie. He home-delivers all day, every day of the week, even if it means delivering just two items late in the evening. The person taking the order on the phone will never complain; seldom will he say, 'No, madam, it can't be delivered today.' If a particular product is not available, he may suggest an alternative that is as good. In India, this service is taken for granted but in how many countries does one find something like this? My husband's American colleague, when visiting stores on a trade visit, found this customer-centric approach 'just amazing'.

Entrepreneurship has received a huge boost in recent years. In my generation, it wasn't as accepted culturally – at least among the people who were well educated and qualified. But in recent years there has been a paradigm shift. Shanti, who is an angel investor, has been in this space for several years and shares her insights:

In the last five or six years, there has been a big change in how people look at start-ups. In the late '90s, Indians went to the US as they thought that was their only choice. That was their aspiration and their dream. What I've seen in the last five to ten years is that *that* dream has changed. I know of people who have left a good job overseas and have taken a conscious decision to come back to India – they've come back because they feel that for the next fifteen to twenty years, India is the place to be. There is a huge opportunity if you want to be part of the entrepreneurial ecosystem and build something disruptive.

The college graduates today also opt out of campus interviews because they want to create and build something of their own. Their aspirations seem more clear and they choose to take the risk at a younger age, build companies in India, solving real problems. There is a lot of passion to contribute to the entrepreneurial ecosystem. At least in Bangalore and the metros, we also see an ecosystem that supports this passion. I think the awareness around start-ups and entrepreneurship is much higher. The government's 'Start-up India' initiative has contributed to building higher awareness and opportunities. India is today the third largest start-up ecosystem globally. I think entrepreneurship is finally being celebrated in India.

In line with the observations made above, here's an interesting finding of a 'Future of Work' global survey conducted by US-based GoDaddy, a technology provider to small businesses, in October 2016. According to it, 60 per cent of Indians working in small or mid-sized organizations want to start out on their own and become entrepreneurs. The proportion of those wanting to start their own business was significantly higher in India when compared to Australia, Brazil, Canada, China, Hong Kong, Turkey, Singapore, the US and the UK.

Creative problem-solving

Indians are resourceful in the face of constraints. They have an ability to find a way out in complex and stressful situations. Rajan says, 'My personal observation is that when Indians are stuck between a rock and a hard place, we are always able to work things out in a creative manner relevant to the situation.' That said, this mindset is often more reactive than proactive.

On a simple or basic level, there is a tendency to 'fix' things. Virginia, who works in the cosmetic industry, says: 'I find people to be very innovative. My assistant has the ability to mend things. It can be something simple like my make-up powder has fallen out – smashed. And five minutes later, he'll put it back together somehow. He's very quick because he hasn't had everything and he's had to operate with limited resources. People are very, very bright, which I don't know whether you'd get back home. There it would be like, "The compact is broken; buy another one," whereas here it's "fix it".'

This is Sangeeta's view on the matter:

> For something we'll have multiple solutions. Because that's what India teaches us. Our life is never straight. You have to go zigzag to reach the end point. Unlike in Singapore or Switzerland, where everything is predictable. Our brains will go from A to Z and, because of that, at times when we come back with solutions on the table, they are all over the place, but they will reach the end point. So quite often we will forget what the processes are as long as we achieve the objective. This is not the case in a developed market, where it's all systems and processes and where people will follow step 1, step 2, step 3 to reach step 10.

The Indian will think and use his imagination. As Shanti points out: 'If you give an Indian a list of steps 1 to 10 to follow, after step 10, he will also do steps 11, 12 and 13. And he will not do step 7 in between!'

Related to the above point, Sateen shares the following:

> If I need something complex to be resolved, I tend to pass the work to my Indian team as they seem to have a more creative

mindset. There is creativity in terms of problem solving, not necessarily process solving. If I need a process set up, I tend to go to China or Hong Kong because they are really good at organizing themselves into a process and then following that process well. In India it's really difficult to make people follow that process. People tend to go all over the place. They are good at getting things solved but not necessarily by using a standardized process.

Because of this ability and flexible approach, Indians may feel constrained when others don't approach problems in a similar manner. An interviewee's opinion, after living in India for several years and being married to an Indian, is: 'One of the things that Indians resent about foreigners is that they (the foreigners) feel that the straight and narrow path is the only one. For Indians, there are always alternative ways and alternative routes.'

Given the above, this chapter would be incomplete without elaborating upon the term 'jugaad'. For those unfamiliar with the term, here's an excerpt from the book *Jugaad Innovation: A Frugal and Flexible Approach to Innovation for the 21st Century* by Navi Radjou, Jaideep Prabhu and Simone Ahuja, published in 2012.

Jugaad is a colloquial Hindi word that roughly translates as 'an innovative fix; an improvised solution born from ingenuity and cleverness'. Jugaad is quite simply a unique way of thinking and acting in response to challenges; it is the gutsy art of spotting opportunities in the most adverse circumstances and resourcefully improvising solutions using simple means. Jugaad is about *doing more with less* ... The word jugaad is also applied to any use of an ingenious way to 'game the system'.

Anand, who has over twenty years of experience in engineering and technology, shares his insights on innovation in the Indian context. He says, 'Indians are very good at taking base designs that come from somewhere else in the world and adapting them to Indian conditions – that's innovation. I think companies that didn't do that failed. If they took a regular appliance made in the US or Europe and applied it in India, it didn't work. A fan made by an Usha or Bajaj typically does much better than an imported fan because they Indianized it to make it more robust for dust, dirt, transportation, field repairs, voltage fluctuations, etc. That's a reason why the Koreans are so successful. They learnt from this and let their Indian teams innovate.'

The downsides

In relation to the problem-solving mindset, Sven makes a good point: 'Very innovative things can come out, but sometimes the result is a cheap and temporary fix that is not as good as a permanent solution in an international environment. Europeans often over-engineer while Indians are pleased too easily. Finding the right balance is the key to success in India and abroad.'

So while creative solutions help in resolving difficult situations, often there are downsides associated with these solutions. A few of them are elaborated here.

Stretching rules

Madhav says, 'Allowing people room for creativity can be difficult in a banking scenario because lots of things are very rule-bound and regulated. So you then have to worry about the intent of the short cut. Sometimes it leads to process improvement, sometimes it leads to a better way of working, but sometimes it leads to creation of risk.'

While the positive of jugaad is that things get done, but differently, the negative is that boundaries are often stretched; one has to be sure that things are done within the legal framework.

Then there is the issue of safety, which an interviewee elaborates on: 'Generally speaking, there is not a good safety culture in India. Obviously we have a very large population and sometimes don't have the same regard for the loss of a human limb or life that you see in the West. Also, safety standards and legislation don't have the same level of penalties as in some other parts of the world.'

Compromise on quality

Things get done but not always at the level at which one wants or expects them to be done. Often the approach is to 'fix' the issue temporarily so that it 'works'. But the big downside is that, in the process, there is a compromise on quality.

Virginia says, 'In our business, we have a lot of people selling us wigs. They look great and they are affordable but they are not 100 per cent human hair. They are 70 per cent human hair and the rest is synthetic. The providers think that they are okay but they are not. They look great for two weeks, after which the hairs start falling out. The approach is to make money in the short term and not worry about the fallout.'

In this context, Anand says, 'If you look at appliances or electrical goods or machines, you will find that often short cuts have been applied. One of the things that we look at is wire harnesses or cable harnesses. Everywhere else in the world, once you set up a process, they will say this is how it is to be done. Every box will be the same. In India, some boxes will have wires that are short, wires that are long, some may have been switched around, and some may have joints or pieces attached. Because it's not seen from the outside, right?'

As Joe says succinctly: 'You can't expect perfection – India is dubbed the land of 98 per cent.'

The desire to see something through to its logical conclusion and finish it well is not commonly seen. The passion for precision, the quest for quality and the desire to excel are not the norm. People often think a job is done when it's only 98 per cent complete! Rajan agrees: 'People will do a very good job to get to 90 per cent, then they will work hard up to 95 or 98 per cent. And they will think this is good enough.'

'Chalta hai'

Literally translated, 'Chalta hai' means 'It works'. In regular usage, it has come to mean 'It's okay'. Okay to be late. Okay to disobey rules. Okay to not get it fully right. Okay to be mediocre.

It is an attitude that permeates all aspects of life. Whether it's roads or buildings, nothing is ever quite finished or finished the way it should be! In the way things are made or in the manner services are provided, there are gaps aplenty. Things are rationalized, excuses are offered. People don't care one way or the other and life continues as normal. If something is reasonably good and works reasonably well most of the time, it is considered acceptable.

Indians in general aren't perceived to be big on discipline. A Swiss expat says, 'In our factory, we had put a process in place and we had people coming from Switzerland to teach the Indian groups. Three months later, the process that was being followed was different! Adherence and discipline are big challenges here.'

In this context, consider Peter's views:

There is a general lack of attention to detail. Partly it's about following rules. I put Japan on one extreme. People there follow rules to a fault. I think Indians tend to have a fairly relaxed attitude towards following rules. The attention to detail in terms of manufacturing and producing, whether it's cars or cameras – Japan has that. Everything has to be perfectly manufactured and engineered. There is that quest for perfection. In India, you wouldn't see that in many places.

The key thing you need in any kind of successful industrial manufacturing facility is attention to detail. And that is so cultural. The Japanese have it in abundance, the Germans have it, the Swiss and Swedes have it, the British don't have it so much, the Koreans have it to some extent, the Chinese don't have it and the Indians certainly don't have it.

How does one work around this?

Indian ingenuity has its positives. But one needs to be cognizant of the associated downsides too. Awareness has to be driven in the organization that cutting corners and compromising on quality will have a negative impact. Rules may have to be enforced to this end. The boss may have to compensate for the team's lack of attention by having a higher attention to the small things himself.

Given the mindset and related issues, how does one work around it? There is no easy way or formula. Sateen shares his approach:

There have been so many times when people have put me in a spot saying, 'It's done,' when it's not done! In technology, there is a concept called 'shift left', referring to the practice of testing a product in the early stage. A lot of Western countries do this but here in India I found it very hard to get that moving — basically getting a developer to test himself rather than giving it to a professional tester. That's why what I found works well is that I start the process off in India and then the quality checking is done by my China team because they are methodical, can find holes in things and are very good at finishing what is started!

This is a challenge, but at least if one knows this, you can compensate for that in any business process through extra quality checks. Because it's anticipated that things will not be fully done or completed well, people and organizations put their processes around this. The downside is that you end up having more people do the same thing, and also spend more time on checking and correcting.

Jaideep Kalgutkar, General Manager at a large IT company, says, 'It depends on us as the consumer whether or not to accept something that is 98 per cent done. If you do insist on a 100 per cent job, you will get it, but you will have to go through some amount of serious effort to get it done and insist on it. I think this will change over time as our people get more exposed to world standards and demand 100 per cent going forward, at least in the big cities.'

Anand lends some perspective based on his several years of experience:

What may be 98 per cent for the consumer on the outside may be 102 per cent for the factory owner or the business. So the guy who uses a little shorter wire is thinking, 'I saved a piece of wire. How does it matter as long as it connects properly? I am saving the company some money.' But for someone looking from the outside, it may violate someone's code of compliance or ethics. So, one has to understand the context.

People tend to generalize without knowing the realities of working with India. It has to be seen in the context of the history of a nation growing up in the 'licence raj' — there was shortage of funds, sub-economic scale of business, scarce resources and efforts to maximize an organization's profitability.

Conclusion

Lastly, here's what Bernard Imhasly, a former Swiss diplomat and foreign correspondent who has lived in India for over thirty years, has to say:

Attention to detail is true and it's not true — like everything in India. There is a popular American business book called *In Search of Excellence*, and I always thought that if I write a book on India, it would be called 'In Search of Mediocrity'!

At the same time, everything in India is so multifaceted. If you look at the world of craft, textile, stonework or woodwork, there is amazing attention to detail and excellence in the most refined form. Plus, there is also the ease that many Indians have with numbers. They can go into great detail. So there is an interesting paradox here.

That's my experience of India — because it challenges your thoughts and judgements. As soon as you have formed one truth, here comes another truth that says: 'No, this is how it is.'

Indians are nothing if not full of contradictions! Attention to detail is not lacking completely; in fact, it can be found in varying degrees across professions and people. That said, there are gaps in the way things are done, but there are positives too. The entrepreneurial Indian is comfortable with numbers, thinks creatively and is resourceful. He is tenacious and aggressive in business. More often than not, he will persist and plod on in the face of competition and adversity. He can stand firm but he can also sway with the wind and adapt. He is resilient and has a big will to succeed. Given half a chance, the Indian will prosper.

A common phrase heard across India is 'Ho jayega', or its equivalent in the regional languages. It means, 'Yes, the job will be done.' But more important than the words is the underlying sentiment: the willingness to try and the hope that things will work – or work out eventually!

7

Negotiating Nuances

When we were living in Manila, a friend's sister visited us while on a trip to the Philippines. She wanted to go to Greenhills, a shopping centre full of interesting artefacts, bags and accessories. I enthusiastically agreed to take her around, not realizing what I was getting into. I am not much of a shopper. I go in and get out of a store in a few minutes, not having much patience to window-shop or look around. Of course, in a new country, you are curious to explore, so you end up checking out things with more patience and time than one would ordinarily.

We were at a huge marketplace. My companion – let's call her Shilpa – started looking at bags and asked for the price. She went to a couple of shops, enquired about the prices of a few bags and then went back to the first shop. And then the fun began. She quoted her price – which was much, much lower than the shopkeeper's. They were taken aback and stared at her as if she was crazy! I saw this and assured myself that this should take just a few minutes, but what I had not bargained for was the way Shilpa bargained.

She raised her threshold price every few minutes, she pleaded, cajoled, alternated between smiling sweetly and walking off, then returning. I had by then switched off, but I saw her returning with bags and I saw the shopkeepers eyeing us with a mixture of exasperation and humour. Unfazed and more confident as she went along, she continued the process with the same zeal and zest. This went on for two and a half hours. Shilpa acquired four bags, many strings of pearls, some table runners, few capiz trays and I had ... a migraine!

This example is indicative of an Indian's mindset when it comes to price discovery – whether it is in the personal or professional space. This is elaborated upon here along with other nuances that are characteristic of Indians when they negotiate. I spoke with people who have vast experience in the area of negotiations – with Indians and across cultures. This chapter contains their insights and things to keep in mind shared by them.

At the outset, let's consider: Do all Indians have similar negotiation styles?

Meera (name changed), an experienced corporate lawyer, shares her perspective:

> In the public sector, you have a very cautious style of negotiating. There is an ability to commit less; there is always a concern that what they are committing to needs a sign-off by the organization and therefore negotiations are 'dryer', less noisy and interactive. They are much more process-driven and therefore take longer. There are some positions which become intractable simply because the relevant person is not willing to go out on a limb and therefore to that extent it becomes a bit frustrating for the counter party.

The other category is that of the promoters. They are nimble, aggressive, noisy, quick and 50 per cent of them, I would say, are fairly risk-taking. What I mean by that is that they are okay with signing a contract and they think, 'We'll deal with what happens next later.' Some who have wider exposure and have worked with multinationals are much more savvy as to what a foreigner is looking for. And they are basically in a position to take decisions and work back with their organization to deliver what they have promised to the counter party.

Then you have the professional employees, who in today's world are much more cautious. Again, it depends on how much they are empowered, how much they are willing to go out on a limb without checking with the ultimate promoter even if they are professionally managed. It's very rare that they will take a decision that will be hostile to the promoter for obvious reasons. But they understand fair dealing, are not stubborn and are able to have a rational conversation.

Negotiating – the Indian way

To get a feel of how negotiations are conducted in India, consider these comments made by a few expats:

'India has many obstacles to satisfactory negotiation of which a Westerner might not be aware. Real estate deals have to run through society agreements; construction has to go through unions; local governments have huge influence. Of course, this exists in places like the US, but it looks different.'

'Negotiations go on forever. Hierarchy and ego play a big role. I find it difficult for people to equate money with value of the product or service. If you want a lower price, you get a less valuable product or service. They don't see it that way. I often double my expectations at the start of negotiations to ensure it's not a total loss.'

'I found negotiations in India to be very similar to those in Latin Europe. Need to work a lot on relationships and form, more than data and substance. It's a gentlemen's display of power.'

Interestingly, the cultural nuances discussed earlier in the book – like the hierarchical mindset, the approach to time and the people-oriented focus – impact the way negotiations are conducted in India. Discussed below are a few characteristics that hold true in most negotiations with Indians:

Indians like to slice

Here's an example narrated by Hari:

One of my all-time favourite stories is of an Indian who goes to a shop that has, on one of its many shelves, '50% discount'. He tells the shopkeeper he wants an item from the non-discount counter but at the 50 per cent discount. The shopkeeper clarifies that the discount is being offered only on the items on the 50 per cent discount counter and not on the others. Not for the Indian. Discussions proceed apace.

Finally, fed up, the shopkeeper agrees to sell the item at a 50 per cent discount in the hope that he would now be able to turn his attention to his other less demanding customers. The Indian is very happy and then, as he is leaving, he asks the shopkeeper, 'Can you give me two for the price of one?'

This is an exaggerated example but the point is taken! The Indian's first instinct is to reduce the price quoted to him, whether it is a personal or professional transaction. The aim is to slice.

But here I would like to point out that people all over the world are cost-conscious; it is not just an Indian trait. That said, the way Indians go about arriving at their preferred price is unique to this part of the world.

And with most Indians, they don't just want to bargain; they also need to, as explained below.

Nimesh Rathod, a business acumen specialist, says it well: 'For Indians, negotiation is more of a need than a necessity.'

In the workshops he conducts, Nimesh devises certain exercises and simulations which his students (who are from the corporate sector) participate in. And he finds that the results are consistent every time: the 'value for money' that his participants get after negotiating and driving a bargain is directly in proportion to how hard they negotiated – how much the seller resisted and how much the potential buyer was able to push the seller. Negotiation is an integral part of achieving this 'value'.

Anand says it succinctly: 'Being fair is a lot more data-driven in other cultures. In negotiations, they are more up front about what they are driving towards. Everybody likes the satisfaction of a deal being closed, but I think the satisfaction of the negotiation process itself is more an Indian thing for sure. It's never about the fact that there's a price for a deal; the fact is you strike a hard bargain for the satisfaction. For instance, "I was able to negotiate harder" or "Look at that, I went along and got this price" – I think that's more an Indian thing. The end values might still end up being the same whether you do the deal in an American, Chinese or Indian context, but how you arrive at that number in the three contexts is very different.'

Which brings me to the question: Are Indians 'value' seekers? It is ingrained in the Indian to seek 'value' irrespective of what he is buying or negotiating to buy. It could be groceries or Diwali firecrackers, a kilo of tomatoes for Rs 20, or state-of-the-art equipment for Rs 20 million! In a lighter vein, an interviewee says: 'Discount is value. We like quality cheaper!'

The quality is often assumed and taken for granted – that it will be delivered and not negotiated, whereas price is. However, from a corporate negotiation viewpoint, while price is an important factor, other factors such as quality, service and reputation also need to be taken into account. Does the Indian negotiator focus disproportionately more on price than on other factors and, in doing so, does he still get the value that he seeks?

Anand puts this in perspective:, 'Unfortunately, I don't think Indians are able to get much better pricing or get a much higher valuation. I think that the negotiation approach is different. Consider the five-hat syndrome: You only want to pay Rs 100 and you want five hats, whereas you can get only one. You will not get the same size hats or the same quality hats. Sometimes in India, people forget that in the thrill of the chase.'

Related to the above, Gaurav Bhatiani, a senior infrastructure professional, makes a good point: 'My opinion is that we don't see the value, we see only the cost. So while we may bargain very hard, we end up with much less than what we think we are getting. I'll give you an example. Let's say you go and buy a television. You bargain really hard and you feel you have achieved a good bargain on a particular brand and you buy it. But what you don't realize is that that brand has no service (centre/arrangement). So if the thing falls apart, you have nothing. You are not buying something only for today but for five or ten years. In my opinion, we bargain hard but we are not bargaining right.'

However, this mindset of being largely focussed on the price may not apply to millennials. They are driven by other factors like ease of use and convenience, not just the price.

Also, it is relevant to point out that while Indians like to slice and bargain, not every deal is negotiated in a similar fashion. Pranav, a senior banking professional, elaborates on this: 'I think negotiation strategies are determined and driven by the nature of the product. For transaction-oriented products in banks and markets, it's "my" price or "your price", or one moves on. Negotiations for long-term contracts, or pitching for a new deal, entail detailed discussions and could carry on for months, if not years. It depends on the nature of the business and the transaction. Sometimes it takes very long to agree on a word or the semantics in a contract.'

It takes a long time

Indians are not a patient race, as is evident from the way people jostle and jump queues and, while driving, cut lanes and continuously honk. However, when it comes to negotiating in the social realm, as mentioned earlier, they have all the patience in the world not only to bargain but also to check out many 'varieties' of the article they want to buy before settling for one. The Amazon 'Aur dikhao' (Show me more) advertisement appropriately portrays the mindset of the Indian customer.

As discussed earlier, meetings can be fluid, given the approach to time. An interviewee, who is an external service provider, often has meetings with the relevant people in organizations to mutually agree on the terms of his service. He shares that he may have planned his meeting like this: thirty minutes to an hour on opening conversation and providing background, couple of hours on technical specifications, an hour and a half on pricing and thirty minutes to conclude. But sometimes, he says, 'These may change, with a three-hour negotiation on price itself!'

As per a paper titled 'The Top Ten Ways That Culture Can Affect Your Negotiation', by American law professor Jeswald W. Salacuse, 'Among the twelve nationalities surveyed, the Indians had the largest percentage of persons who considered themselves to have a low sensitivity to time.'

During a negotiation, an Indian can keep slicing and time can continue to dilate. But not always, says an experienced lawyer: 'It depends on where you are and who is the Indian in question. If you are in a professional set-up, time is valuable. A promoter who has all the time in the world to get the best buck is less stressed about time. But generally speaking, after a while, the counter party also gets fed up and the negotiation becomes counterproductive.'

In public sector organizations, one of the reasons people don't take decisions quickly is that they don't want to be held accountable if something goes wrong in the future, and hence they want alignment with or a sign-off from all possible stakeholders. This takes time.

Nishith Desai, an international lawyer and globalization expert, says: 'Senior people in the organization may not commit in a negotiation. They will continue to negotiate and the process goes on for a long time. Even for lawyers, what happens is that culturally, at times, it becomes important for them to show their presence. So there is an argument on every comma and every full stop! Also Indians are always argumentative, which again means that negotiations get protracted. People on business trips to India should not assume that they will be able to close something in one day!'

The 'R' factor matters

As Meera puts it, 'Indians like a relationship that goes beyond the negotiating table. They would like to take you to dinner, sometimes they would like to invite you to their family home, and it's quite common to see reasonably good bonds build up during the negotiations and then carried through.'

That said, the relationship factor may not matter as much at the onset of a negotiation. Indians may go about cultivating the relationship differently from some of their Asian counterparts. They may not invest as much at the start – like scheduling formal or informal lunches and dinners – but they will do it along the way.

We discussed the two categories of trust – cognitive and affective – earlier. Affective trust is a requisite component in many emerging markets, including India. There's no denying that a good working relationship breaks barriers and helps align expectations of the parties concerned.

So what are some implications of the relationship-focussed approach in negotiations?

In his paper, Salacuse points out that different cultures may view the purpose of a negotiation differently. While for some cultures the primary goal of a business negotiation is a signed contract between the parties, for others it may be the creation of a relationship between the two sides. In his survey of over 400 people of twelve nationalities, he found that whereas 74 per cent of the Spanish respondents claimed their goal in a negotiation was a contract, only 33 per cent of the Indian executives had a similar view.

In view of the above, it may be worth considering how one's counterparts view the purpose of a negotiation and work around that.

An interviewee, who is experienced at handling cross-cultural negotiations, says, 'In other places, there is a clear understanding that a scheduled lunch or dinner is for business purposes. Here, it isn't always clear whether somebody is inviting you for business or just like that, given that Indians are relationship-driven. Whereas in other countries, it's more focused towards business outcomes, here the outcome is not a must.'

An expat, who is a director of a large organization, shares his observations about the implications of the people-focussed approach:

> The negotiation is all about relationships. So, when people want to negotiate with you, they will build a relationship. And that's what they focus most of their energy and effort on. Once they've got that relationship, they think it's done and dusted and it's forever. It's not a good or bad thing – that's the way they do it. It's not so much about the price or terms or benefits.
>
> If they stop performing from a business aspect, they will always expect the buyer to tell them in a nice way 'Your prices are too high' or 'Your quality is not good' or 'Improve this or do that'. They will not lose the business because the relationship is more important than the actual service. It's not a bad thing. But it takes a lot more time.

This could result at times in capability not being given the consideration it merits. 'Because relationships are important in India, a lot of negotiations are done based on relationships and not just facts and logic. This doesn't apply when one is dealing with a large professional organization that is credible and has a huge reputation. But it could be relevant in other cases,' says Rajan.

Gaurav, who has over two decades of experience in policy, financing and strategy, sums it up well:

> I was representing a foreign agency, so the processes and systems were very well laid down and there were not too many exceptions or different ways of doing the same thing. Whereas on the Indian side, it wasn't like that. That's because of the cultural difference between how India and some other countries work. In India, relationships are definitely a factor in a negotiation. That applies to the public and private sectors and even to multinational corporations that are largely staffed by Indians. Despite the fact that their parent organization may have much stricter rules, their Indian subsidiary will have a lot of relationship-based dynamics.
>
> In my opinion, if a negotiation is happening between people you have known for a long time versus people you have sat down or met with only for the negotiation, there are two aspects. One, the probability of reaching a closure with a person you have known is dramatically higher. You will be able to have far more give and take, more communication and so on with that person. Two, this is somewhat subjective, but a good negotiation is where both parties end up feeling that they got what they wanted out of it. They are happy, a win-win.
>
> My sense is that when there's a relationship in place, when communication is more open and transparent, you will achieve closure more often, you will have happier outcomes and a higher probability of win-win situations.

Discussion and deliberation

Indians like to discuss before, during and after a negotiation! But, at times, there may be reluctance to sign contracts even at the end of all the discussion.

Understanding lengthy contracts may be a factor. Nishith Desai puts this in perspective:

Even today, when an Indian reads British or American contracts, it's not very easy for them to decipher. They run into pages and pages! Also, Indian business people, who are not exposed to the world or those who do not fully understand the terms and clauses they contain, may have an inherent fear of signing contracts. So, a handshake deal is sometimes easier to strike than signing. In general, the habit is not to sign something in a hurry. They will ask one person, then ask somebody else. However, over a period of time, Indian companies are learning new terms and trends. The fear of the unknown drives their behaviour; new-age contracts are more difficult for them. But after some experience, they begin to understand and streamline their negotiation.

The other factor that could explain the reluctance to sign is: what is the value of the contract? If somebody breaches the contract, one's only recourse is going to court. This will take ten to fifteen years. So, why sign a contract? Instead, people think that if there is a good relationship, that will work better. They will sign contracts because they have to have a legal document. But they will rely on their gut to do business with you. Because contract enforceability is an issue.

This is to be viewed together with the point made earlier, that is, the negotiation may be less focussed on having in place a watertight contract and more on agreement on the general direction, broad terms, and fostering a good long-term association.

Another interviewee puts it differently: 'People are not wary of signing contracts – as long as they can negotiate their way out of them! The contract signing is the first step, then there's a discussion *after* that – that's also typical. Which is where there is a mismatch culturally. Indians love to negotiate even after the deal is negotiated.'

Meera says, 'More than go back on the word, sometimes we tend to change our mind a bit too late before the contract is signed. So, you've agreed all along to a particular position and suddenly, in the penultimate draft, you say "the deal terms don't work for me". That creates anxiety.'

It may be relevant to mention here that in general, Indians prepare less and do much more on the fly. Also because of the complex and uncertain business environment, there is a preference for some flexibility and open-ended terms. This is not just in India but in many emerging markets where things are dynamic.

Styles of communication

When negotiating across cultures, differences in styles of communication can impact the successful conclusion of negotiations. Here is an example of this shared by David, a Swiss expat, who worked for many years in India in different capacities:

We were negotiating a contract with an organization in India. I was in discussion with the Indian businessman; we had been negotiating for a couple of months, back and forth. And finally a meeting was scheduled to conclude the negotiation with the chairman of the company in Switzerland.

It went on the entire day and, in the evening, my boss, who was not in that meeting, got a call from a board member who told him, 'We concluded the contract.' Since my boss and I were at a

restaurant when he got this news, we celebrated this achievement
with a glass of champagne and were happy that we had reached
the target we were intending to reach.

We had planned to meet the Indian gentleman the following
day at a hotel in the heart of Zurich. We met him and greeted him
with 'Congratulations that we could finally reach an agreement!'
And he said, 'What congratulations? I never gave any consent.
I expressed my will that it might be possible to reach an
agreement.'

You know, communication from the Indian side can be, 'Yes, I
can do it, maybe it's possible,' and the Westerner understands
this mainly as a 'Yes'. Eventually the deal went through but not
at that point of time! This was quite difficult for us as it was a
misunderstanding and I had to pull the two ends of the rope
together. And that was quite an exercise because it was a
misunderstanding at a high level.

As pointed out in the chapter on communication, the 'Yes' is
not always a 'Yes'. While Indians can be direct in communicating,
they aren't always so. They are expressive and can be quite noisy,
but in general they don't seek to confront.

As an interviewee says, 'I think we don't like to say things
that are very cut and dried for fear of losing the point or losing
the deal or for fear of confrontation. So, we nod our way and
hem and haw. And then leave it to a lawyer or an accountant to
give the bad news.'

It's relative, though. Compared to some cultures, Indians
are very direct. Consider the example below. An interviewee,
who worked in a Norwegian company, shares his experience of
being part of their team that was in the process of negotiating
with Indians:

As an Indian, I was part of the Norwegian team negotiating with an Indian company, our partner. I was supporting the negotiation, not leading it; my Norwegian colleague was leading the discussion. There were noticeable differences in communication styles and approaches. The Indians were more direct, while the Norwegians were reluctant to say what they want. Even within the organization, the boss may not tell a subordinate exactly what he wants. For example, he may say, 'Hello, you may be interested in investigating this issue.' So, during a negotiation, if he tells an Indian, in his own understated manner, that 'this may be of interest', there is a good chance that the Indian will forget it; he will not consider it as central or important to the negotiation. That then becomes a challenge.

In this negotiation, a question was asked, but a different one was being answered! For example, a simple clarification on a data point sought by the Norwegians resulted in a long answer relating to the history of development in India and challenges related to working in the infrastructure sector! I realized that there were gaps in understanding on both sides.

Sometimes the Norwegians took offence to something that was totally unintentional. In one instance, one of the Indian team members said something to the effect that they wanted more than a 50 per cent share since they had worked and contributed more than 50 per cent on this transaction. While this was known and agreed in principle, it wasn't liked at all by the Norwegians, as they may have wanted it to be given as a favour and putting it directly may have hurt their sentiments. Finally, in this transaction, the offended Norwegians walked off.

I asked my interviewee, in such a situation, what advice he would give the Norwegian team or a non-Indian. He said: 'One thing is to talk more directly, of course. Also, there is some investment required by our expat friends in order to understand how Indian organizations work and how they negotiate. Many times, Indians don't have a fully formed position when they begin the negotiation. So, people not familiar with these nuances have to spend some time understanding them. Also, perhaps the front-ending should be left to an Indian. Otherwise what may happen – and I saw this – is that good projects and deals fall apart on account of cultural gaps.'

The aggressive Indian?

Given the Indian's penchant for bargaining hard, are Indians aggressive while negotiating?

I spoke to some experts, who have played an active part in negotiations, and asked them for their views. This is what they had to say:

Gaurav says, 'From what I've seen, I wouldn't say that we are too pushy. We may appear to be so as we are not well coordinated. So, different people asking for different terms in the same deal sounds pushy, but it doesn't mean that we want all of that. We want some of that but we haven't prioritized or coordinated between ourselves. We are fairly direct but not as direct as some other cultures are, but I wouldn't think that we are too aggressive.'

As to whether Indians are argumentative, that's not really a question! Indians like to peruse, analyse and over-analyse. They are good at finding flaws in arguments.

Meera remarks, 'Yes, the Argumentative Indian is definitely a stereotype. We are constantly looking for bargains, discounts. That's just our nature. I don't think, as a stereotype, Indians are aggressive or pushy. Indians want to get the deal done. So, to that extent, if one wants to call us pushy, that's okay. But I think we are nimble as a race. We can trade, we can give and we can give in. And, of course, if one is just an A-type personality, one is aggressive!'

Nishith fleshes this out well: 'We are very argumentative in negotiations, but I do not know about being very aggressive. When you say aggressive, it means you are trying to extract more. I would say that aggressive means, 'These are my terms, I am not going to accept anything else.' But if aggressiveness means sticking to one's terms, that is not the case with Indians. The way negotiations happen is that initially people will over-pitch the price. And then they will come down. Because most of the time in India, price discovery is a challenge. There are no benchmarks, no studies, so if you want to find out what the price of real estate is in an area, you will get a range that is very broad. The rate in one building may be Rs 4,500 per sq ft, and five buildings away it may be Rs 3,000.

People will immediately compromise, a little bit here and there. There is always a little give and take which is not the case elsewhere in the world. People are more flexible; they are constantly arguing, bargaining and negotiating. Everything is an oriental carpet deal.'

The negotiation with Mr Sharma

Lastly, here is a real-life negotiation that Anand was involved in. He shares his experience and learnings:

'We were negotiating with a family-owned conglomerate, which was in a bit of financial difficulty, to acquire a subsidiary that had a manufacturing business. The person I was dealing with, let's say Mr Jain, based in Hyderabad, was a pleasant, mild-mannered person. Given that the deal was worth over

Rs 100 crore, and considering the various complexities involved, there was much discussion. We had been going back and forth several times over six months until we reached an agreement that we both felt comfortable with. However, since Mr Jain was the second in charge at the company, he indicated that this agreement had to be approved by his boss, whom we can refer to as one Mr Sharma, who was based in Delhi. Of course, that was fine with me and we set up a time for my American boss to fly down and meet with Mr Sharma.

'The expectation was that it would be a courtesy meeting and we would have a handshake and signature followed by a celebratory dinner. But, to our surprise, Mr Sharma began on an aggressive note by questioning the strategic rationale of the deal and the basis of the price that had been negotiated with Mr Jain. He was quite animated, and at one point got up and started walking around the room talking about selling the family jewels at a bargain. We tried explaining and then turned to Mr Jain for help, but he looked down and didn't say a word. I realized that we were on the verge of derailing the deal, so requested my boss and Mr Jain to give me a few minutes alone with Mr Sharma.

'I spoke to Mr Sharma respectfully in Hindi and told him that I understood how difficult it must be for him to part with a business that had been started by his father. I told him that we would be good for the business and would bring new technology to the market. I did not mention the price. He replied in Hindi and asked me to bring my boss to his house for dinner that evening.

'From the perspective of my boss, it was a very frustrating meeting and he felt that Mr Sharma was being very unreasonable. Anyway, we went back to the hotel and firmed up our strategy for the dinner meeting. The plan was to stick to the agreement we had with Mr Jain and not negotiate on the price, but keep reiterating how we would bring new technology to the business and build on the market leadership.

'We landed up for dinner at Mr Sharma's posh place in south Delhi with a bottle of Single Malt and the evening started off with Mr Sharma personally pouring us drinks at his bar and showing us various family pictures on the wall. Over the next three hours, he was at his charming best. He spoke about his trips to the US, his time spent in the manufacturing facility as a young man and his plans for rebuilding the family business. Several times he tried to revisit the price and we stuck to our script. Finally, after about three hours, the dinner was coming to an end and we were still uncertain if we had a deal or not. And suddenly Mr Sharma said, "Okay, I agree to your price," and he shook hands with my boss. And that was that!

'Some takeaways I had from this encounter were:

- It's never over until it's over. Mr Jain had given us the indication that the deal was ours. So, my American boss in particular was more taken aback than me since he had taken everything at face value. In India, there is always room for manoeuvring, even after agreeing. Never count the deal as done until you sign on the dotted line.
- Always know who the final decision-maker is. In this case, we assumed that Mr Jain was empowered enough; it turned out he wasn't. Mr Sharma was in the driver's seat and wanted to determine if he could negotiate a higher price. It was his father's business and there was an emotional connection.
- There was probably a bit of an ego issue too. By letting Mr Sharma have the last word and showing him that we would be good for the business, we were able to get the deal done.
- There are cultural and regional factors at play too. At the risk of stereotyping, a different approach may be needed

while dealing with someone from Delhi compared to someone, say, from Mumbai or the south of the country.'

Conclusion

These are some insights and advice shared by people who have been involved in negotiations with Indians:

1. One important thing in the framework is that both parties agree to the methodology. That's important because otherwise it's like potatoes, it could be anywhere from Rs 15 to Rs 30. How do you decide? In that context, people now get an investment banker or some intermediary to help evaluate this.
2. In negotiations, the hierarchy factor comes into play. For instance, during a negotiation, it is expected and accepted that people will give respect to the senior persons in the room leading the discussion. Seniority can be leveraged to close the finer points of the deal, and facilitate smoother outcomes.
3. The non-verbal piece is important. Indians are not very good at keeping a poker face. With some cultures, you can't tell what they are thinking. But Indians are more transparent in their body language.
4. Look over and beyond the contract and its terms. Before signing on the dotted line, it's important to get a sense of whether the person or organization one is negotiating with is one you will feel comfortable working with over the period of the contract.
5. And be ready to walk away. A lot of people get caught up in the thrill of the chase or get offended.

6. Be patient but firm too. The non-Indian party can draw certain boundaries and highlight the areas where compliance is more important.

7. Go easy with the contract. First, cultivate the Indian party, agree on the broad principles and then get into more details. Second, get the basic documents or contracts in place which will be non-binding, like an MOU, so that there is a good framework to work with; then get into the more detailed documents but make sure you use simple English. If you try to rush, the other party may get on the back foot. Gain trust and confidence first.

8. Understand who the decision maker is, otherwise there will be surprises in store.

9. Unless you see a contract, or an order, you cannot say that the deal has been done.

10. Get a good adviser who understands cross-cultural nuances. Don't expect the mindset to be like yours. Be flexible.

The Indian is complex, driven by different nuances. Those shared in this chapter offer a peek into his psyche. But things are changing in this area; negotiations are now getting savvier and more professional.

As a lawyer observes, 'Slowly, people are becoming more business-like, people are learning as they work in other parts of the world. Also, in the last ten years, a lot of Indians have repatriated here after studying and working overseas. They have a good understanding of negotiation techniques and strategies. They know how business is done globally, so we will see a change in the attitude and behaviours in the next ten to fifteen years.'

8

The Return of the NRI

Ravi left his hometown in south India to pursue postgraduate studies in the US. Thereafter, he followed the usual route of getting a job, getting married and 'settling down'. Fifteen years into this happy existence, he learned of an interesting job opportunity back home. After some deliberation and soul-searching, he decided to move back to India with his wife and kids. He had his share of naysayers; he ignored them. After all, India's economy was looking up and this would be an exciting time to be in the thick of things.

A month after the move, Ravi was having his favourite drink of caramel frappuccino at a Starbucks outlet in Delhi (something he couldn't have imagined doing in India ten years ago), wondering whether he had taken a decision that would adversely affect his professional life, his family's growth and happiness. Had he done the right thing in moving back?

This is not a unique situation. The world over, repatriating is a delicate process, both challenging and comforting. Like any transition, it requires considerable adjustment, a reassessment of priorities and, not least of all, a positive outlook. That said, the complex and chaotic nature of the way things work in India, coupled with the cultural nuances and social expectations, add to the difficulty of this transition.

Dear fellow Indians who have repatriated, this chapter is dedicated to you, keeping in mind your predicament. We take a look at some of the challenges that you may face and also highlight the positives – because it's not all bad!

Fitting in: In general and professionally

This is one of the first hurdles you may encounter. From all outward appearances you may look, dress, talk and behave like a regular Indian on the street, but you are, in fact, quite different.

The Indian who isn't quite

While it's tough for the returning Indian who has lived overseas for a few years, it's tougher still for the Indian who has lived all his years outside and has visited India on occasion. He may be familiar with Indian customs and practices but only in theory, or to the extent these were followed or shared by his parents. He may not have a larger contextual understanding. He may or may not be conversant with Indian languages. If he was born in the US, there is even a terminology for this person: ABCD or the American-born Confused Desi. Notwithstanding this, because he is Indian, he is expected to behave and think like one.

An expat, who saw how his Indian colleague tried to fit in, shares his perspective: 'An Indian repatriating here has more challenges than a foreigner, especially if it's someone who more or less grew up and was educated outside India. Everyone expects him to be Indian, but basically he is not coming here with that complete Indian value system and way of working. People expect him to speak Hindi, understand the context fully and navigate his way comfortably.'

On account of the above factors, for this category of Indians this chapter may not be as relevant as the rest of the book!

The Indian who moved back after some years

Now let's consider the case of the Indian who has been overseas from the time he went abroad for his undergraduate/postgraduate studies or on work. He may have spent many years adapting to the ways of a different culture, which would have shaped, developed and probably changed him as a person. Notwithstanding this, he is expected now to reintegrate naturally and seamlessly.

While the people he meets on moving back may appreciate his work experience or qualifications, that is usually the extent to which they can relate to him. If they haven't been in a similar situation, they cannot and do not think how different his life may have been, and how he will now have to readjust and 'fit in'. In fact, if they were asked, they would in all probability say, 'What's the fuss all about? He was out for some years, must have had a great experience and now he's back. He knows how to manage here; after all, he's one of us.'

If you are a repatriating Indian and have supportive colleagues, friends and relatives, good for you! If not, accept the situation and move on. Quickly. You might want to take some time adjusting to the way things work, like most expatriates or foreigners do when they move to India. But the system may not afford you the luxury of gradually settling down. In these respects, it is harder for a repatriate than a foreigner. But in other ways, it is easier to fit back in your home culture than making your way into a new culture.

This is what an Indian who has worked overseas for seven years says of his initial days back in India: 'I think on one level there's been no difference. I started my career in the same organization, so a certain familiarity was there which made it easy compared to somebody who may be coming back to India but is new to the organization. In that sense, I would say it was not that challenging; in fact, I felt very welcomed. Somebody would introduce me to their team saying, "Hey, here is the person who interviewed me X years ago!" So I have had that warmth from my colleagues. I felt quite at home.'

However, fitting in on a personal front may be a bit different, especially if one is not working.

Fitting in: Familiarity and friendship

My personal experience was that it's not as easy to make new friends as you would when you were overseas. There, one is in the same boat with other foreigners mutually seeking new friendships. I recall the time when we had moved to Manila, in a high-rise overlooking the golf course and the sea. In the first couple of weeks, every time I came across people in the elevator or at the poolside, they would smile and invite me to their house for a chat and a cup of tea. In a new and alien land, this warmth helped us settle in.

After many years of being welcomed and similarly welcoming other expats who made Manila their home, we moved back to Mumbai – once again living in a high-rise with a sea view. Here, the conversation would typically go like this:

'So you guys are the new people who have moved in! Where are you moving from?'

'From the Philippines; prior to that, we were in Singapore for some years.'

'Oh, Singapore is so nice and comfortable. Which city are you from in India?'

'We are from Mumbai.'

'So you are from *here*. Great that you are familiar with this city.'

Elevator door opens. Conversation ends.

Of course, not everyone has this experience. But in general, given the fast pace of life in the metros, this kind of hurried chat is fairly common. People don't feel the need to reach out, assuming that while you are the new kid on the block, you have enough and more friends and can find your way around.

A friend, Aditi Vijayakar, who repatriated to India from South Africa a few years ago, narrates her experience:

Moving back to India as a trailing spouse, you are not in the 'expat circle' since it is assumed that, being Indian, you will know enough people and blend here very easily. If your old friends have moved out of the city, the ones who have been here for years have their own families, their own friend circles and are fairly set. And you are not working right now because you don't know how long you are here for. So when anyone looks at hiring you, they don't know whether this is a short-term arrangement or if you will move out after a few years. It leaves you thinking that technically you belong to the city, yet you don't belong!

However, despite the change, Mumbai is still a fairly easy-going place – it's easy to settle in. You can find your own space and live where you want and be who you are. You can always find places that you can go to and things that you can do in terms of theatre or music or movies.

Professional challenges

An executive who moved back after some years overseas feels that he has less flexibility at work than when he was abroad. This is what he says:

> I had a lot more flexibility overseas. I would manage my own time. Here, I have to keep my boss in the loop about what I am doing if I am out or not at my desk. It's not as bad as it probably sounds but there is a difference. For example, overseas if I was out for a lunch meeting which went on for a couple of hours, when I came back, my boss wouldn't bother because he trusted me to be responsible. Here, if I'm not at my desk, it's assumed that I am away on personal work. It's not said explicitly, but it's an underlying thing and it's across levels.
>
> My experience professionally is that I feel I have taken two steps down. I don't think one's overseas experience is valued as much as one thinks it should be. And I wasn't given as many responsibilities as I had hoped for; people aren't thinking of how to utilize my experience. They have something in their mind and they try to fit you into that whether that's a good fit for you or not.

Rajesh, after being used to working in a structured system abroad, discovered that on coming back, there is a new 'normal':

> Aside from your day-to-day job, your energy goes in worrying about very basic stuff. As a bank, providing services such as online and mobile banking, we can't have outages as people need to access these. But they can't because sometimes the links are down! Or suddenly you have a situation where the chief minister

has died and people are emotional in the city, so nobody will go to work. How do you explain this to somebody?

Three weeks ago, there were some disagreements around a festival. How do you tell your overseas stakeholders, 'Well, I am going to shut down today, you are not going to get supported because people are fighting over who will catch hold of the bull!'

The systemic inefficiency impacts one's productivity in India. According to Madhav, who was based in Hong Kong earlier, 'Planning for meetings has to take into account traffic, travel and quite a few external factors. For instance, if you have to fly down to Bangalore for the day, you can at best do three meetings. You can't plan the way you would in Hong Kong. Coming from a very efficient Asian country like Singapore, Hong Kong or Japan, that is very difficult to get used to.'

In order to get around these aspects, people end up working more than they did in places which are efficient and predictable. This in turn results in a skewed work-life balance, also compounded by longer commute times.

On the personal front: Challenges and positives

The day-to-day living challenges like incessant honking, traffic snarls, pollution – all of this can be, and is, stressful. And there are some things you get used to and take for granted when you are abroad, only to find that they aren't here. For instance, a friend misses access to good parks or gardens to take his kids to. There's the aggression on (and off) the road, the jostling, the constant chaos.

Aditi says, 'If you are used to a more efficient life abroad, when you come back to your home country, it's like lowering your benchmarks yet again. It's difficult to do mentally. It's just this whole thing of accepting that this is how life will be now.'

So in response to the inevitable question that people ask of most repats, 'Weren't you used to this growing up?' the answer is, 'Yes, we were, but when your benchmarks have changed, to readjust and recalibrate once again takes time.'

Here's what a repatriate shared about day-to-day living after coming back to India:

> On the office front, everything is professional. But on the personal front, there is a lot of unprofessionalism that you have to deal with because a lot of the unorganized sector is really unprofessional. Like the real estate broker. All he did was introduce me to the landlord, get me the contract and go with us for the lease registration. The attitude was: 'You deal with it.'
>
> In the US, for example, when you go to the house, the broker would have inspected every single thing – what is not working, what is broken. He will make sure that everything is fixed. Here, it's been four months since we moved into the house and there are things that are broken and still not fixed!

Another area that could be challenging is that of managing household staff. The reason this finds a mention here is that a repatriate's sensibilities, after years of living away, may be different from that of Indians living here. A small case in point is that of a repat's wife, who finds it difficult to hire a cook as she thinks they are not as mindful of hygiene as she had grown used to abroad. This despite the fact that they have only been away for six years!

Then there's the matter of social expectations. When one is living overseas, social interactions are usually limited to friends and colleagues. On moving back to India, one may be faced with expectations to regularly meet extended family members, many of whom one may have lost touch with. For people who enjoy this kind of socializing, there's nothing better than to be back here. However, in many cases, this entails making adjustments with respect to how one is used to spending one's time, especially given the nature of family obligations in India.

This was experienced by Chloe, who lived in the US before moving to India a few years ago: 'When I got here, my dad, who is of Indian origin, said that there are expectations involved in being part of a big family. He would tell me, "You need to go visit this person." And to me it didn't make a lot of sense. Now that I've been here four years, it does make a lot of sense because of the emphasis Indian culture places on relationships and on fulfilling and sustaining those connections. But it took me a long time to understand that.'

On a related note, repatriates, used to spending their leisure time in a wide range of ways while overseas, find that there are limited recreational options here. As one person pointed out, 'Recreation means going to clubs, restaurants or somebody's house. But these are passive, whereas overseas it was activity-driven and we would do a lot of things outdoors on weekends, like driving to places or even scuba-diving!' However, consider a different perspective: Mukesh finds that his personal life has got much richer after repatriating as he has the opportunity to associate with political causes and start-ups.

As discussed above, there are challenges but there are also positives. A huge one is the emphasis on relationships. Returning to India to spend time with parents is a huge plus emotionally. This is usually a significant factor in the decision to move back home. An added bonus for Indians whose kids have spent many of their formative years overseas is to see them reconnect with family back home. Also, it is a given that growing up in India, with the many experiences it provides, equips one with many life skills.

My husband and I moved back to India when our daughter was twelve. Given that it was a critical age, I was worried how she would adjust to life in India. But, surprisingly, she took to it fairly well – to a great extent because of a good school. Over the years, I have seen her become more confident in navigating her way around, forming her own connections with her cousins and making new friends, all of whom have lived in different countries. It is heart-warming to see her connect not just with the extended family but also with the city and the country – that is very special for a repatriating parent.

There's the comfort of knowing that no matter how annoying, unpredictable and intrusive life can get, you are amongst your own people. In your own country. Surely that accounts for something despite all else!

And, of course, perhaps the best thing about moving back is to be able to savour those delicacies that were a big part of your childhood. Food is sacred to Indians and is often their raison d'être! The restaurants overseas may be capable of whipping up your favourite fare, but they seldom come close to *that* taste you can recall! At least in my case when we moved back, this was one of the highlights for me – returning to this taste of home.

Conclusion

This is an excerpt of a conversation I had with Rajesh:

Me: Are you happy to be back?

Rajesh: It's all right (laughs). Coming in, I knew there would be a quality-of-life trade-off. But I came for the work. My assignment is exciting; from a professional standpoint, this is the time!

In conclusion, while there are professional and personal positives, there are challenges and trade-offs too. It is a mixed bag, and the way one approaches it is crucial in determining whether the stint will be a positive one.

There is no formula or strategy that works to make your return and integration smooth. Patience helps, as does making a few friends who are in a similar situation or who have weathered this before. As days turn into weeks, and weeks into months, you will have got close to mastering the art of managing your way around. And one of these days, you could be the go-to person when a dear friend moves back to India and needs some advice!

9

Sugar, Spice and Some Advice

From expatriates and repatriates, here it is – living and working in India in their own words, coupled with some advice to make the ride smoother:

'It's different – accept it'

Temper your expectations because people who are really excited have the most difficult transitions.

- In order to survive in this country, you have to, first of all, accept the 'otherness' as being normal and not apply your own yardstick.
- Don't copy-paste your country on to India. Don't expect India to be like the place you've come from. It's never going to be. Accept it. If you moved here from Singapore, you're never going to make the Indian population you work with Singaporean. Come hoping to blend in.
- Don't try to force people to do things that you believe to be right. There are a billion-plus people doing things in a certain

way, and it might be wiser for you to adjust to their way rather than telling them that they are doing everything wrong.

• Adapt, but you need not lose your identity in doing so.

'It's not easy (here) but your life will be what you make it out to be'

People complain all the time about moving to India. They have to be clear what their goal is and why they are here.

• With about 50 per cent of our families, the mums and children don't want to leave India when it's time to leave, because they found their way in a city where they never expected to find their way!

• You can't sit within the four walls of your new home and think, 'Oh, this is an unfriendly city.' You have to find ways and means of getting out and making friends. You need to be positive about whatever life here offers.

• You have to tolerate what's different and try to make the best of both worlds. In the beginning, most of our friends were expats. Now, 50 per cent or more are Indians. That's why we feel very comfortable in our daily life.

• Let the non-working spouse also work or volunteer, let the entire family be involved and adapt to India. We moved here when my wife also had a job.

'Dive in. Let yourself loose. India can offer some great cultural experiences.'

Don't bring any preconceived notions; there can be polar opposites in India for any situation. It's almost like a different continent with its diversity and complexity.

- Be open to everything. India is just so full and there is just so much to learn and it's such a complicated place! Try to meet as many people as you can, experience and explore the country as much as you can, learn as much as you can, and just try to soak it all up. Because India is a place like no other. I know because I have lived in so many other places; there's no other place in the world that's going to be as vibrant!

- India has so much to see and explore. Unbelievable cities and remains of a glorious past. The culture is so different and so intense that it is impossible to get bored.

- There is so much going on, it's intense. Go to as many festivals as you can – Diwali, Ganpati, Durga Puja, Eid – because that is again so unique about India: the diversity of these festivals.

'Connect, connect'

I think if you don't mix in with people here, you'll miss out hugely on Indian life. Even if you don't like cricket, go to a cricket match. If someone wants to take you to a classical Indian dance, just go. Because you never know what you will learn. Do you want to go and see Ganpati immersion on Juhu beach in Mumbai? Go. You'll learn never to go again! So smile, be open and when someone says, 'Would you like to go?' say 'Yes'.

- My advice on the professional front would be to communicate as much as possible to understand the culturally different approach to work and interaction in this country. This will open doors for smoother collaboration and working together.

- This is my formula wherever I go in the world and I strongly believe in it. There are always common points. You need to find those. The minute you find those, you connect with people.
- Take the time to listen, understand and connect with as many people as you can. Don't go for an empowerment model too early. Let people feel comfortable before doing anything.
- Take a genuine interest in the other person's family because if you do that, it creates a lot of rapport and people respect that – where do they come from, what are the names of their children, how long have they been in this environment, etc.
- If you are able to connect with your team emotionally, the commitment they will bring to your organization will be very high. If not, they will just come and do a job.
- In other places, you would say, 'Let's do it this way,' you discuss it once and it's done. Here, you need to often understand how people are feeling and how they are doing. The socialization aspect is not to be underestimated.
- As in most places in Asia, you need to adapt when you are delivering a particularly difficult message or nasty feedback, as the loss of face following such a situation could be more pronounced than one may be used to.

'Patience is a huge virtue'

- Be patient; nothing is going to happen with the snap of a finger!
- With infrastructure issues, whether it's your wi-fi or roads, you have to accept that it's not going to be smooth.
- On the professional front, it's learning on the job. Be aware of time and time management.

- People need to adjust their work style and then go with the flow.

'It's not necessarily a straight line'

- The most important thing is to be able to deal with ambiguity. If you are looking for clarity in any stakeholder engagement – be it the government, clients, staff – it's going to be a nebulous environment. Because it's culturally like that.
- On the professional front, be flexible, but not too flexible. Expect delays. Extend yourself to help others. Build strong personal relationships. Don't take things too seriously. Negotiate on some values. Stick to the important ones. Understand that you will meet the best of people and the worst of people.
- In the office, the look and feel could be similar to offices around the world. But in the country, you'll likely see organized chaos!
- Don't over-analyse or question things because sometimes it's not going to make any sense whatsoever. But you're not going to change it, so just accept that *that's* the way it is.
- If you expect punctuality in office, also consider external logistical factors like where and how far people live and which train lines they take.
- Spend more time preparing prior to almost every meeting (for example, whom you are meeting with, who the head of the organization or department is, which part of the country he is from, etc.). Also, when you walk into a room, be mindful of whom you shake hands with first.
- You need to come to India with strong ideas and convictions and a lot of energy. When you have to implement something,

you need to be convinced that it's the best thing in the world. And then you need a lot of energy to implement that. You could be surrounded by people saying it's not the right thing to do. And you are the only one thinking it's the right thing. So you need to be very strong, otherwise you can't survive.

- People may ask you about your religion, orientation, anything – you can't get offended. You have to get used to some loss of privacy. Or at least get used to dealing with questions. You can continue to maintain your position in a polite manner, saying you don't discuss personal questions.

- You have to design a team much more carefully in India. Abroad, perhaps you don't have to give it too much thought, but here you have to make sure there aren't too many superstars in the same team or too many overlapping agendas.

- It's important to develop a Plan B and C.

'What you see is not necessarily what you get'

- Don't take everyone at face value. The person who is polished and talks well and is savvy may not be the guy who does the work or who has the power. Understand that it's not that straightforward.

- The concept of karma is an important thing to understand in the Indian context – that things are not just here and now. People have long memories; do not do business based purely on transactions – it's not a one-time deal.

- Have an open mind; stand in the shoes of your colleagues to see their perspective.

'What I like about India'

- Sunny weather, working with young people and the vibrant and dynamic environment. You don't get that level of enthusiasm and energy elsewhere!
- The hunger for learning and the positive attitude towards turning the country/business around.
- The passion of the people; they are incredibly intelligent and immensely loyal. There is a dichotomy as they also want to succeed personally, so if you can get both of them working, that's great!
- The perspective/outlook on life is much more positive. The middle-class segment is growing, people have a lot of ambitions. Sometimes there's too much (ambition), so that's a challenge here.

'If you want to be successful in India, you need to be able to want to live here'

In India you can't separate work and personal life as much as you can in other places. There's so much richness and colour in all aspects in this culture. If you were to just see it as a job, first of all it would be a waste, because how can you not just soak this up and enjoy it? In the country I lived in earlier, we would interview interns who wanted to move there on their technical skills and if they could do the job. We didn't quiz them too much on the external environment, but I have found that here you really have to. It's important to get a sense of how comfortable people are, or will be, in the environment outside of work. It is more complicated here!

'Don't shy away from it: it could well prove to be one of the most memorable chapters of your career!'

- For an expat coming here for a term of two or three years, don't look at it as a finite period of stay. Come in with your eyes wide open as there is a lot of value, lots to learn. People who have lived here longer are happier.
- Look at the positives, harness the capabilities of the team rather than being too worried about the negatives.
- The people are energetic, bright, well educated, hardworking and generally cooperative.
- Here you need to put in more effort and enthusiasm than in other countries. But after that you can probably live a much easier life in other countries!
- When you repatriate, you should clarify with your new bosses what your role is going to be and what exactly is expected out of you. Take the plunge only if this is acceptable to you and if you have the clarity after taking the ambiguity out of the picture.
- I find professionals in India to be on top of their game. The HR leaders I've worked with know their stuff. I've really had to up my game working here because everyone at the management level is a subject matter expert. While the school system may not encourage critical thinking, it has enabled people to retain lots of information and, after years of experience, to process it quickly.
- I can see some incredible talent. I've come across more people with a higher intellect here than anywhere else.

'I learned to appreciate in India that not all things are black and white'

Some people just can't adjust. I am not sure if you can prepare that well – people have to live through the experience. Things can be hard, time-consuming and frustrating. I wish I was told – there's going to be a learning curve, be patient with getting adjusted. My best advice would be: jump in with both feet, realize that it's going to be unbelievably complex and nuanced. You're going to get slapped in the face, miserable at first, overwhelmed but will love it at the end. Just give it time before you write off the experience. You can't know it till you live it. There's a depth to the life experiences and relationships you establish. Anyone who spends some time in India is fortunate. They'll accomplish and achieve so much.

- My bosses ask questions like: When will this be predictable? How can you anticipate that? And then you have to explain to them that you cannot anticipate that! And they get uneasy and ask you how they can support you with resources if you don't know what's going to happen. India is challenging, and what may be true today may not be true tomorrow. So that lack of certainty will remain in this environment. India has taught me that it's not all black and white.

'Let it go!'

For me, when things were different in India, there was a lot of judgement on my part in thinking American culture was better. One is not willing to shift one's perspective on things like 'Why do they take long chai breaks?' It's always, 'They do it *this* way', 'I am used to it *this* way' – which is better? And almost always the way you are familiar with is going to be your answer because you understand the whys. I think for many expats, they want familiarity so much. Acknowledging that it's different doesn't mean that one is better or one is worse. I kind of regret the judgement because there's so much that I've missed out on that could have opened me up a bit more.

- I've learnt – and it's an acquired skill – to let go of a lot more stuff. Enjoy the process. Don't be too attached to specific outcomes. Go with the flow.

- Living here has certainly helped me appreciate how lucky I am. There is a great disparity of wealth in India and it's really in your face all the time. So it's certainly given me appreciation of my place in the world. And hopefully my child will get the same appreciation.

- I would say that if you are coming here, try and stick around people with a positive attitude to life. Not the people who bring you down.

- You have to be like a fish. You can either swim against the stream or you can swim with the stream. If you're going to swim against the stream, you're going to wear yourself out and get exhausted. You can't start telling people how India needs to run. You may have thoughts about that but don't think that you're going to make a change in the way India is. Because you will be miserable if you go around trying to criticize and fix everything.

- Embrace the experience with a sense of adventure, being prepared for the unexpected!

- I think the learning has definitely been to look at things differently. That's a constant learning because you think, 'Oh yeah, I know this,' and then you still get surprised!

'You can find a way to get anything done!'

- And this isn't necessarily work related. If you need to buy something or need something fixed, there is always somebody who will know somebody who will know somebody who can do it. And it can be done at any time of the day. And it's just amazing – that relationship and networking thing is incredible and I think it's what makes this country amazing. Because things can be done in ways that you would never think possible!

Sense and sensibilities

The new expatriate boss once hosted a luncheon for people from the office, mostly local staff. And he had this very fancy new caterer. So the meal was non-Indian, served in three or four courses. I was on vacation but my colleague told me that the lunch, being a sit-down affair, took a long time, people were served small portions and they had to eat with forks and knives, which a few of them may not have eaten with earlier. And so overall it didn't seem so positive.

Later, I asked the boss about whether the people in the office had liked the food; I mentioned that I understood some of the office boys may not have eaten with silverware earlier, so they had felt a little uncomfortable. To which he replied, 'Well, at least I am glad that I gave them that experience because otherwise they may never eat with silverware.'

> And I thought, 'What are we trying to accomplish here? Do you want to accommodate people in their own culture? Because we are guests here. Or do you want to bring our culture and expose them to it?' And it's probably both at the end of the day, but it's a fine line. And here's the point: for Indians, food is so important! What's the point if they don't enjoy it?

- Expats, especially Western expats, have this bad habit that whenever something unfavourable happens, they associate it with the chaos of India. I think it's important to be cognizant of this tendency and get over it quickly. What I mean is that they go to the airport and the flight is delayed and they say, 'Phew, that's India.' To which I often say, 'Have you ever flown in the US?' But here very often a sink will break and they will be like 'India!' No, it's just a broken sink, sinks break everywhere!

- Be willing to ask naive questions. When we first got here, we had an elementary school paediatrician giving us health advice, and one of his tips was, 'Just use common sense.' And I raised my hand and said, 'Well, my common sense is very different from yours because I grew up in a different place. Common sense for me is I can go to the sink, fill it up with water and drink it. If, during the monsoon, I am wearing flip-flops, do I need to go home and wash my feet?'

- Talking to expats who have been here for a long time helps. They probably end up being your best resource because they are cognizant of both worlds. Or find an Indian who went to university overseas. I found that was really useful; he had a sense of my sensibilities. In so far as I understand India, he understands my country!

'Develop a network outside of your work'

- The quicker that happens, the better. I know some people for whom it's their church, for some it's their pickup basketball league, and for others it's yoga. If your only friends are at work, you feel that you have only two worlds: home and work. Even if you are out with your work friends, you need something else.
- People want to just keep to their comfort zone. And I think they are really missing out.
- Let's face it: we all live in a bubble in India. For some, the bubble is small, for others it's a bit bigger!
- A friend used to say: 'Anyone who says that they are unable to find something in India or are unable to engage in something that they wanted to and were used to is lying.' If you used to be part of the Philharmonic Orchestra, you could do it here; you used to be part of the opera, you can do it here. If you've not found it in India, you're not looking in the right place; you've not asked the right people. Who can illustrate this better than Nick, a trained mixed martial artist, who was extremely passionate about fighting when he moved to India as a full-time history teacher? In his leisure time, he was able to not only find a group of people who practised this sport but was also offered an opportunity to coach them, travel with them to international competitions (where they were the first Indians to win foreign titles in this sport) and even helped set up a world-class fight gym here – all the while teaching IB History to international school students! In his words, 'It's been amazing!'

'Embrace India for what it is. It will change you for the better.'

And to end the chapter on a note that encapsulates the most important lesson about working in India:

> We do an exit survey with employees who are leaving and we ask them, 'Which of the following fifteen characteristics do you feel were most important for your success as someone coming into India?' And the number one characteristic that emerges every year is: Embracing India.

10

The End of the Journey

India, with its contrasts and contradictions, can be overwhelming – to an outsider coming in, yes, but even to Indians who have lived here all their life. But despite the polarities and the pluralities, what is also evident is the amazing energy, indefatigable spirit and the zeal to do more. That is the hope at the end of the tunnel – the belief that anything is possible in a country of over a billion people.

While cultures are diverse and people are different, universally there are some core things that people value and cherish in varying degrees. For instance, at the workplace, people would like to be respected and motivated. They appreciate teamwork, recognition and good compensation. They want to believe their job is part of contributing to something greater. But when working in another country and in another culture, understanding nuances that are particular to that country and culture helps. Knowing how India works and what makes Indians tick, and understanding how to leverage the strengths and manage the gaps can be the difference between success and failure when working in India.

This book has been a step in that direction.

By being cognizant of the factors and nuances that operate in the Indian business environment and learning new ways of doing things, one can improve one's experience of working in India from 'all right' to 'great'! In any move across countries – or even when working in one's own country – it helps to be aware of the nuances of the work culture at play, and it's really about taking the good with the bad.

For people who are used to order, structure and discipline, India is the antithesis of all of that. It is chaotic, noisy, difficult, with every possible thing that could go wrong going wrong. But, as one interviewee said:

'In the end, it all works.'

Acknowledgements

My sincere thanks to the people I interviewed for this book: Amit Agarwal, Charles Bacon, Brian Bade, Sateen Bailur, Gaurav Bhatiani, Martin Bienz, Josh Bishop, Brendon Breen, Mary Chowdhury, Peter Clark, Susanne Cox, Sven De Wachter, Nishith Desai, Rahul Desai, Michael Enderle, Michael Evangelista, Mary Kay Hoffman, Virginia Holmes, Jos Hulsbosch, Bernard Imhasly, Bhasker Iyer, Craig Johnson, Justin, Jaideep Kalgutkar, Madhav Kalyan, Chloe Kannan, Imrana Khera, Rajan Khorana, Nick Kilstein, Yuk Dong Kim, Joe King, Stans Kleijnen, Eric Labartette, Lorna, Zia Mody, Shanti Mohan, Deepshikha Mukerji, Rory Newcomb, Robert Oates, Melissa Pain, Jeetu Panjabi, Nimesh Rathod, Chris Rogers, Anand Sanghi, Hari Sankaran, Mark Schamp, Amy Sebes, Ali Sleiman, Mitsuru Tada, Kanchana TK, Carrie Udeshi, Richard van der Merwe, Joop Verbaken, Aditi Vijayakar and Ashish Vijayakar.

Thank you in equal measure to five people who didn't wish to be named. Thank you all for generously sharing your views and anecdotes because you believed that they would make a difference to those who read this book. Not only did you all bring in your own flavour to this book, I learnt something from each one of you!

* * *

This book for me is the pot of gold at the end of the rainbow. There have been many people who in their own unique way contributed to this book. I am thankful to:

My husband Amal, for supporting me while I wrote this book and in the journey of life. The most positive and balanced person I know, he helps me see the stars and reach for the moon.

My daughter Anushka, for being my sweetest and tallest blessing. May she continue to smile and shine.

My parents, for the safety net of their love and protectiveness, and for always being there.

My in-laws, who have always been supportive. I know this book would have made my father-in-law proud.

Tania Leger, for introducing me to the field of cross-cultural training. She ignited an interest that took me on a whole new journey.

Amit Bhartia, with whom the idea to write this book took shape, and who continues to encourage, inspire and enthuse.

Arti Dwarkadas, for saying 'yes' and kick-starting this project.

Ranjit Shahani, for his positivity and generous support from the time I commenced work on the book. From the kind introductions to a few interviewees to his encouragement while I plodded on, it was only fitting that the Foreword is written by him.

Meenakshi Sanghi, for being my go-to person while writing this book. Her balanced perspectives on what worked, what didn't and how it could be changed were extremely valuable.

Parag Jain, for wading through my initial drafts and for his 'helicopter views' that helped sharpen my writing.

Gayatri Durairaj, for her belief in the book and for letting me tap into her infinite pool of encouragement and positivity.

Jitania Kandhari, for her insights, and for inspiring me to raise the bar in writing and in life.

Manish Gupta, for his guidance and resources that helped me navigate the world of publishing.

Kanchana TK, for graciously connecting me to people who contributed to the making of this book.

Anupriya Divecha, for her unwavering support no matter how far-fetched the request.

Purvi Sheth, whose organizational skills and friendly advice could always be depended on.

The Writers Club at the American School of Bombay, for their suggestions and comments.

Deepa Bhartia, Anshu Bhartia, Priya Kini, Kalyani Ajrekar, Manoj Jain, Nimesh Rathod and Harsh Mehta, for their kind support and encouragement.

Prashant Dhumal, for painstakingly printing and organizing the numerous drafts and transcripts.

Sharon Nachnani, for her efficient organization and logistical support.

And Siddhesh Inamdar, Commissioning Editor at HarperCollins, for believing in this book from the beginning. I am grateful for his vision and commitment. His edits, which gave the book its final shape, made it 'work'.